THE ULTIMATE QUEST

A GEEK'S GUIDE TO (THE EPISCOPAL) CHURCH

T0268439

THE ULTIMATE QUEST

A GEEK'S GUIDE TO (THE EPISCOPAL) CHURCH

JORDAN HAYNIE WARE

ILLUSTRATIONS BY TYLER LOLONG

Church Publishing
NEW YORK

Copyright © 2017 by Jordan Haynie Ware
Illustrations © 2017 by Tyler Lolong

All rights reserved. No part of this book may be reproduced, stored in a retrieval system, or transmitted in any form or by any means, electronic or mechanical, including photocopying, recording, or otherwise, without the written permission of the publisher.

Unless otherwise noted, the Scripture quotations contained herein are from the New Revised Standard Version Bible, copyright © 1989 by the Division of Christian Education of the National Council of Churches of Christ in the U.S.A. Used by permission. All rights reserved.

Scriptures marked KJV are taken from the KING JAMES VERSION (KJV): KING JAMES VERSION, public domain.

Church Publishing
19 East 34th Street
New York, NY 10016
www.churchpublishing.org

Cover art by Tyler Lolong
Cover design by Jennifer Kopec, 2Pug Design
Typeset by Rose Design

Library of Congress Cataloging-in-Publication Data

Names: Ware, Jordan Haynie, author.
Title: The ultimate quest : a geek's guide to (the Episcopal) church / Jordan Haynie Ware ; illustrations by Tyler Lolong.
Description: New York : Church Publishing, 2017. | Includes bibliographical references.
Identifiers: LCCN 2016041207 (print) | LCCN 2016048730 (ebook) | ISBN 9780819233257 (pbk.) | ISBN 9780819233264 (ebook)
Subjects: LCSH: Episcopal Church.
Classification: LCC BX5930.3 .W37 2017 (print) | LCC BX5930.3 (ebook) | DDC 283/.73—dc23
LC record available at https://lccn.loc.gov/2016041207

Printed in the United States of America

for derek, my questing partner

Contents

In which we explore that which is contained therein

Acknowledgments

No one is alone, as Sondheim says, and any good adventurer knows she is nothing without her party. As such, I have so many people to thank:

My amazing editor, Sharon, who took a chance on a first-time author, and whose sage advice (with the occasional "what's that from?") helped make *The Ultimate Quest* as clear and as helpful as it is. (All mistakes that remain are mine, of course.)

Tyler, illustrator extraordinaire

The best beta readers and cheering section: Brin, Josh, Kelli, Robert, Matthew, and Eli

The "game guys," who introduced me to Pathfinder and weekly put up with me comparing the game to church stuff: Jay, Kim, Mike, and Paul

My parents, who taught me that reading is the key to everything

The tireless women prayer warriors of the "God Thread"

Derek, best of men and best of husbands

Introduction

In which an adventure begins

[This chapter introduces geeks to the world of church. For church folk seeking an introduction to the realm of geekdom, "Introduction 2.0" on page 7 will offer some party tips.]

So you want to go to church. Good for you. If you're between the ages of eighteen and twenty-nine, you're already ahead of 65 percent of the population. Further: Church is awesome. Not only do you get to meet lots of really cool—and nerdy—and countercultural—and comfortable in their own skin kinds of people, but you also get to experience the life-changing, well, there's hardly another word but *magic* to describe the transformational experience of piercing through the veil that separates heaven and earth, joining the heavenly chorus, and partaking of the very body and blood of God in the Holy Eucharist.

Geeks and the Church belong together. Christians thirst for adventure, have a sense of destiny, and desire to participate in something bigger than oneself as much as any questing gamer. The geek's obsessive need to understand how something works, to read the manual, to build a complex vocabulary that explains precisely what's going on, these are traits that particularly the Episcopal tribe of Christians have in spades. We both form intense community bonds, we affect nerdy insular jargons, and we view change with suspicion.

The problem is, like most of geek culture, church (especially the Episcopal Church) can be pretty impenetrable when you first encounter it. This isn't necessarily bad—there are rewards to be found in the effort it takes to understand the centuries of history and theology that underlie the symbolism embodied in the liturgy found in your local Episcopal Church. We geeks like having *some* barriers to entry. We're the rules lawyers, the ones who've studied the Player's Handbook for years, the ones who figure out the exact schematics and comparative sizes of the ships in *Battlestar Galactica*, *Star Wars*, *Star Trek*, and *Firefly*. The ones who argue continuity issues, who write fanfiction, who have the best Star Wars puns in the Dagobah system. So we are definitely capable of learning the ins and outs of Episcopal liturgy.

The first question is: Why do we want to? Well, assuming that you want to go to church, and assuming that you are a geek (and you did pick up this book), understanding how and why we worship the way we do is part of your identity. Episcopalians have always been a people who value common prayer over common belief. During the Reformation (mostly sixteenth century), instead of writing dense theological tomes like his contemporaries Martin Luther and John Calvin, Archbishop Thomas Cranmer wrote a Book of Common Prayer. So if you want to understand Episcopalians, you have to understand how we worship. And why wouldn't you want to understand how we worship? Nobody likes feeling out of the loop and confused when somebody suddenly drops to their knees in front of you as you're trying to walk down the aisle.

But now that we've decided it's a good idea to learn all these signs and symbols, how do we do it? There's not exactly a Player's Handbook for the Episcopal Church. There *are* online forums where people can argue the rubrics (that's *rules*; we're starting the vocabulary lesson *right now*), but they can be pretty intense. You need an introduction—a hitchhiker's guide to help you figure out how to get the basics under your belt so that you can join in the conversation. That's where this book comes in.

This book will introduce you to the greatest Adventure Path ever written: following Jesus Christ. Now, before you write me off as unbelievably sappy, hear me out. What is the Christian life if not some Lawful, Neutral, and Chaotic Good folks trying to follow a quest? We're the scrappy outlaws with hearts of gold, the tortured moral leaders trying to make decisions for the tiny remnant of humanity left after the Cylon attack, the last airbenders trying to restore balance to the world. The thing is: we know the odds are long, C-3PO. They're so long, in fact, that we will certainly fail. But Jesus deliberately failed for us, by allowing himself to be killed on a cross. Reinhold Niebuhr (a very fancy theology person who happens to be President Obama's favorite moral thinker) talks about how Jesus's ultimate failure "transvalues the world's values"[1] and makes this failure the ultimate victory. Remember that line on James and Lily Potter's grave? "The last enemy that shall be destroyed is death."[2] It's actually a line from Paul's first letter to the Corinthians, where he declares that Jesus's death *has* already destroyed death, and we are guaranteed eternal life through his saving grace. Not if we're good. Not if we believe in him, in the right way, as expressed by some preacher who *totally doesn't have his own biases or anything*—no. Jesus has destroyed the last enemy, death, and we no longer have anything to fear.

But still we're on this quest, and enemies do surround us: but on the inside, not the outside. We have met the enemy and the enemy is us. Greed, anger, pride, lust, selfishness, laziness, pettiness, vengeance—all these prowl around us hapless adventurers, offering us the opportunity to give up following the Jesus Way. How do these enemies still exist, when the last enemy, death, has already been destroyed? Welcome to the *already but not yet*. We'll talk more about that in the "Magic: The God Part" chapter [check out page 119].

Now: There are more ways to follow this Adventure Path than the Episcopal way. Lutherans, Roman Catholics, Methodists, Quakers— they all have their ways of following Jesus that are ancient, respectable, relevant, and theologically sound paths to God. This book will make some points that they (and others) will agree with. But the Episcopal way of following Jesus is a particular way—most often, a particularly geeky way. We have archaic rules that we love to argue about. We have what one friend from another Christian denomination has called the "best words." We have rectors and thuribles and monstrances and chasubles and all the rest and the other thing. We dress up every Sunday, and our worship, more than any other I've encountered, feels the most alien—the most other-worldly. Church in an Episcopal way is the ultimate role-playing game: a chance to get out of your skin and touch a world that's not your own.

This book will help you get a foothold in that world. It will define some of those scary terms. It will help you understand what, exactly, you're getting into. Think of this as the instruction manual you read before booting up your PlayStation; the inside of the box of *Settlers of Catan*. It will help this brave new world open before your eyes and enable you to participate fully in these strange, otherworldly rituals. There's a "Choose Your Own Adventure" element to it—each chapter will let you know where to turn next to follow your interests.

Who am I, to make such a claim for this book? Well, I'm a geek. Like, legit. I read all the Star Wars Expanded Universe before I was fourteen. I took fencing in college. I play D&D—*Pathfinder*, actually. Be it a 14th level ranger, a 16th level sorcerer, a 6th level rogue, or a 2nd level warpriest, I can roll dice with the best of them. *Firefly* got me through my Peace Corps service, and *Battlestar Galactica* through seminary. I know this stuff.

I know the church stuff, too. I'm a priest. I've got a whole degree in this. I've argued cassock versus cassock-alb with the best of them and rules lawyered my way through General Convention (the Episcopal one, not Gen Con) in 2012. I know the difference between a *cappa nigra*, a cope, and a collarette. I know why clergy shirts are (usually) black. I know how many times the Lord's Prayer appears in the Book of Common Prayer (fifteen or twenty-five, depending how you count).

So come with me on this quest. Familiarize yourself with this world, and I promise you'll make the next Knowledge (religion) check. To paraphrase Captain Hook, "To die might be an awfully big adventure, but to die to self and live again as Christ's new creation is the biggest adventure of all."[3]

Introduction 2.0

In which the adventure is further explained

 [This chapter introduces church geeks to regular geek stuff. If you've got a passing familiarity with the differences between *Star Wars* and *Star Trek*, you own a PlayStation or Xbox, and/ or have played a tabletop RPG, you can probably skip to "The Hero" on page 11.]

Let's be honest: The Church is not cool. I'm sorry if that bursts your bubble, but it's true. Following the way of Jesus is life changing, transformative, adventurous, fulfilling . . . but still not cool.

Fortunately, there is a community out there who is used to being uncool. And it's a community that seeks a transformative life of adventure. A life built around the power of story. A life that fulfills you more as you devote yourself more fully to it. This community is usually known as geeks.

Now, you may not consider yourself a geek, dear church (wo)man. You may think of yourself as cool, calm, and collected. Maybe you were a jock in high school. Maybe you're a leader in a trendy industry six days out of the week. Maybe you were a beauty queen prior to discerning a call to Holy Orders. But I have to tell you: The Episcopal Church is full of geeks. Certainly the pews are full of geeks in the traditional sense—those queuing up to see the latest Marvel film or rolling dice at a weekly *Dungeons & Dragons* night—but worshipping God as an Episcopalian is, in some ways, inherently geeky.

Like much of geek culture, church (especially the Episcopal Church) can be pretty impenetrable when you first encounter it. This isn't necessarily bad—our symbols are richly laden with heritage and meaning that is worth preserving. Plus, doing the hard work of digging into this quest can be rewarding. And geeks like having *some* barriers to entry. As major fans of intricate worlds, they're used to studying rulebooks, figuring out the exact schematics and comparative sizes of various and sundry starships, noticing continuity errors, writing fanfiction, and making spectacular puns. In short, geeks are an ideal audience for diving into the complex liturgical theology that they will encounter at an Episcopal Church.

> A quick vocabulary lesson: nerds typically = smart; dorks typically = socially awkward; and geeks typically = obsessive fans of genre fiction in literature, television, video games, and comic books. Now, there's obviously some overlap here. A lot of geeks are smart, a lot of nerds are socially awkward, and a lot of dorks like sci-fi/fantasy stories. Don't get too hung up on the differences. But this book is written for, and plans to talk to, geeks.

Geeks and the Church belong together. We both seek the adventure that comes from pursuing a mission bigger than our own personal destiny. Geeks have an obsessive need to understand how something works, to read the manual, to build a complex vocabulary that explains precisely what's going on, just like Episcopalians. Our communities are tightly knit, we speak a strange, unearthly tongue, and we view change with suspicion.

This book is written for geeks, and for Episcopalians who want to relate to geeks. And why wouldn't we? With Comic-Con attendance numbers and comic book movie ticket sales soaring, the success of *The Big Bang Theory* and the fame of Lin-Manuel Miranda, geeks comprise an enormous group of people who need to hear the Gospel. They follow and inhabit fictional worlds, they connect emotionally with fictional characters, they are drawn to the power of fantastical stories—and we can offer them the Great Story. There's a "Choose Your Own Adventure" element to this book, so you can skip the parts you already know in order to connect more deeply.

In order to share our story, we have to be able to connect with their stories. This book hopes to aid you in that translation. So here's a quick vocabulary lesson to get you started as you level up in your understanding of the geek community:

n00b: A newbie, or someone who is new at this. A lot of geek speak reflects computer lingo and comes from online gaming communities. It reflects a certain keyboard style that may be unfamiliar to, well, n00bs to the community. n00b can be used derogatorily or affectionately, depending on how much your newness is messing with someone else's gaming experience.

XP: Experience points, earned as you leave your n00bhood behind and complete portions of your quest. Every so often, you gain enough XP to . . .

Level up: At various points, you gain enough XP to add a new level to your character. In geek quests, this is usually once you've found enough treasure, killed enough bad guys, explored enough territory, and you gain new skills and better weapons as you go.

RPG: Role-playing game. These games can come in video or table-top varieties, but they always involve building a character and completing a quest as that character. The best-known tabletop RPG is *Dungeons & Dragons*, but there are lots of other varieties in that vein.

DM/GM: Dungeon Master/Game Master. In tabletop gaming, this person controls this adventure. They "run" the game, setting up encounters for the characters, interpreting rules, and playing all of the bad guys.

PC/NPC: Player Character and Non-Player Character. A Player Character is played by someone sitting at the table/video game controller, a Non-Player Character can sometimes be controlled by the player(s), but is designed by the DM or gaming system. NPCs are usually allied with the player(s), but watch out for sudden but inevitable betrayals![1]

Alignment: Players can choose their own moral code. There are two choices of three: Lawful, Neutral, Chaotic and Good, Neutral, Evil.

The next several chapters will take us through the basics of church: the Book of Common Prayer, vestments, going to church, the person of Jesus. Come and see the Great Story reflected throughout geek culture. And if you still get stuck with the lingo, there's always "Worlds Unknown" to clarify things on page 155.

The Hero

In which Jesus Christ is Lord

 [This chapter introduces you to our hero, Jesus Christ. If you already know him pretty well, skip to "The Ultimate Quest" on page 14.]

To every generation is born a Slayer, one girl in all the world.[1] But Christians believe that in all of history, there has only been one Savior, and that is Jesus Christ, the Lord. You may not realize just how familiar you are with the story of Jesus. But geek culture is full of heroes who follow the story of Jesus Christ as they save the world. These stories, intentionally (J. R. R. Tolkien)[2] or not so much (Joss Whedon)[3], express the sacrificial love of God written on our hearts so indelibly that we can't help but retell the story, whether or not we follow the Way of Jesus.

> So let me tell you a story. It is an ancient story. One that goes back to: *In the beginning,*[4] before the Earth and the Heavens existed, before anything that was created and had its being, God was. And in the beginning with God was the Word. Begotten, not made, by God, the Word existed in the beginning with God and in God and as God. Together with God and with the Word was the Spirit, brooding over the waters of the deep. Together, these Three who are One created all that is—all that we can see, and all that we are only beginning to perceive, and all that we have absolutely no idea about. On Earth, the Three in One

> Some scientists claim that the universe has up to twenty-two dimensions. We can only perceive three (four if you count time). So there is a lot more going on out there in the universe than we know.

God created human beings in the image and likeness of God. In the image of God they were created, male and female he created them. Each and every person you meet bears the image of God. God then chose human beings, and particular human beings, to have direct relationship with God, the Creator of the Universe. Abraham answered the call of God and left his homeland for the Land of Promise. Rebekah listened to God's word and ensured the transmission of the Covenant. Moses spoke with God face-to-face, and left those conversations with his own face shining.

But evil was afoot in the world. Selfishness, pride, envy, corruption, anger, lust, and wickedness drew God's people from the love of God and led us to betray one another. The first murder came between brothers and left their mother bereft of children. Men handed their wives over for abuse at the hands of kings lest they be killed for refusing. Slavery arose as prosperity became more important than people. And the world continued to deteriorate as the Sin-beast won battle after battle.

Just when all appeared lost, a messenger appeared to a young woman behind enemy lines. He shared with her a daring plan: the Son of God would become human. He would become her son too, taking human form from her body. This would merge God's divinity with our humanity, equipping our fragile frames with the ability to escape the power of the Sin-beast. It was a dangerous quest, one that most would refuse. But the woman, Mary, agreed.

Nine months later she bore a child and named him Emmanuel, God with us. But usually he was known as Jesus of Nazareth. Jesus grew in wisdom and in years, and when he came of age he proclaimed that a new kingdom had arrived in our midst. As he traversed our world he inaugurated that reality by his teaching, the performance of miracles, and building relationships with those deemed weakest and worthless by the world. But the Sin-beast arose once more. It could not bear the threat he represented. Jesus's message that the last shall be first, that love is stronger than fear, that forgiveness trumps law observance offered a different way of life, free of the Sin-beast.

Voices began to clamor for Jesus's execution. People questioned his fidelity to tradition, his humility, even his sanity. Once Jesus took up the traditional mantle of a prophet by riding triumphantly into Jerusalem, the religious leaders of his time had had enough. His violent cleansing of the Temple and proclamation that he had the authority to throw out the moneychangers became the final straw. The Sin-beast infiltrated Jesus's inner circle in the person of Judas Iscariot. The powers that be (the human ones, not those seen in *Angel*)[5] convinced him to sell Jesus out. They arrested him, and turned him over to an authority even greater than themselves: Pontius Pilate, the Roman procurator of Judea.

Egged on by a people frightened of change, Pilate had Jesus beaten, and sentenced him to die. But what none of them knew—what even the Sin-beast had forgotten—was that Sin and Death are connected. Neither can live if the other does not survive.[6] And Death could not survive the death of the Author of Life. Jesus, the Son of God, was simply a size category too large to enter into Death. Death exploded trying to contain him. He burst the bars of Death, carrying with him that humanity with which he had been equipped by his mother Mary; carrying with him *our* humanity. And when he triumphantly returned from the grave, he opened the gates to eternal life to us as well.

This victory sealed the final fate of the universe. The Sin-beast's power has been broken, forever. And yet. And yet. The battle continues against the forces of Sin and Death. They have not accepted defeat, and they still prey on the redeemed, beloved people of God. As we await the day of Jesus Christ's glorious return, we engage the enemy as we are able: we protect the weak from the strong, we seek the gain of others instead of ourselves, and we love even those enemies whom we are fighting.

This is our hero, whose example we follow. This is our quest.

The Ultimate Quest

In which the reader accepts the quest to follow the Baptismal Covenant, guided by the wisdom of the Book

 [This chapter speaks directly to the covenant we undertake as we pursue our quest: the Baptismal Covenant. If you remember your baptism well, skip to "The Player's Handbook" on page 21 to learn how to read the questing guide. To learn more about why we make this covenant, go back to page 11 to learn about "The Hero."]

The first thing a gamer needs to do is to build her character. This is something non-gamers don't realize about tabletop, role-playing, and video games: It involves *lots* of prep work. You can't just show up and make it up as you go along. Any sensible gamer will have spent time looking through the Player's Handbook to determine their character's race, class, weapons, and abilities. In some games, it's important to have a backstory for your character, to find out how he came to be with this party of characters and what his motivation is.

In the Church, we have something similar. Some traditions will get mad at me for not listing the Bible as the Player's Handbook. Lord knows, all doctrine and practice comes from Scripture, and some books of the Bible offer practical advice for how best to live as Christ's community on earth. But I think the Bible properly belongs in the role of backstory, or introduction to the Adventure Path here. The Bible is not (merely) a rulebook or even a guide for God's people; it is the story of God's love affair with the world. God created a whole world for the pleasure of it, and then chose a people called Israel out of it to be a particular Chosen. Out of that tribe, Mary was commissioned to bear God's Son, Jesus Christ, who would redeem the whole world from Sin and Death, under whose rulership we had fallen. Jesus did so, through his Incarnation, Crucifixion, and Resurrection, [Jump to "Magic" on page 119 if you need to unpack these comments now, or wait and keep going here.] and then sent the Holy Spirit to sustain us, to guide us into all truth, and to sanctify us as we journey on our quest toward the kingdom of heaven.

Why capitalize the word "Church"? Capital-C church refers to the whole Body of Christ, as it has existed throughout time and around the world. It's universal. It includes all Christians that ever have been and ever will be. It's not a building, and it's not limited to one denomination—the Church includes Roman Catholics and Lutherans, Orthodox and Reformed, Disciples of Christ and United Methodists. Lowercase-c church just means that building with the steeple on it around the corner.

The Bible chronicles that story. It sets the scene. It outlines the world in which we live. Sure, there are some tips for living in that world the Jesus Way (let's call them Rule Zero), but the real Player's Handbook, at least for Episcopalians, is the Book of Common Prayer. The Book of Common Prayer lays out the norms of interacting in worship, establishes the roles of each class (called *orders* in the church) [see "Classes" on page 45], and guides the Christian through everyday life. It interprets the Bible for modern living. It provides us with a lens through which to see. No Christian can survive without frequent re-readings of the Bible; how else can we make sense of the scary and confusing world that surrounds us? But the prayer book is our handbook, our guide, our everyday companion.

So what's in it? Well, first, it's got a calendar that lays out a different way of ordering the days and hours than the regular, mundane, secular way. There are prayers for individuals and groups, then the two greatest adventures (or *sacraments*), Baptism and Eucharist and lots more minor ones.

About those classes. Every PC in the Church is a minister. And what is this ministry? What adventure are we called to do? Paul writes to the Corinthians,

> From now on, therefore, we regard no one from a human point of view; even though we once knew Christ from a human point of view, we know him no longer in that way. So if anyone is in Christ, there is a new creation: everything old has passed away; see, everything has become new! All this is from God, who reconciled us to himself through Christ, and has given us the ministry of reconciliation; that is, in Christ God was reconciling the world to himself, not counting their trespasses against them, and entrusting the message of reconciliation to us. So we are ambassadors for Christ, since God is making his appeal through us; we entreat you on behalf of Christ, be reconciled to God.[1]

So we are all called to be ministers of reconciliation, and to be ambassadors for Christ.

But what does that mean? How can we do it? Christ has a mission, a quest for us that needs doing out in the world. But before God sends us out, we are given some gifts: the grace of forgiveness, the Holy Spirit to comfort and provoke us, and, most importantly, we are given one another, incorporated into Christ's own mystical body. Then God requires some promises in return. We promise that we believe in God: Father, Son, and Holy Spirit. This is largely a question of alignment and of deity. In this Adventure path, only Good-aligned characters will do. You can be Lawful, Neutral, or Chaotic, but the God who made all Creation declared that it was Good, and so we shall be. For those of us who like to be the Good Guys, this is awesome news. For the gamers who prefer to play evil aligned characters, I've got some bad news for you: That is not allowed in this game. Furthermore, we can't be just any Good character; we promise to be aligned with God the Father, the Son, and the Holy Spirit. Since God is the one sending us on this quest, this is eminently reasonable. We can ally with Good creatures who hold a different deity on a number of different quests—and indeed we should, for all that is Good ought to stick together—but the Ultimate Quest, striving toward the Kingdom of God, requires our allegiance to the God who made that Kingdom.

After our alignment is settled, God asks us for five commitments to the quest. These are the five things we have to do every day as part of our quest. The good news is that God knows and expects we will fail at these and, like Gandalf, will hopefully shake God's majestic head at us and give us another chance the next day. But that does not relieve us from the responsibility of trying.

These commitments are:

Continue in the apostles' teaching and fellowship, in the breaking of bread, and in the prayers.

The apostles' teaching can be found in the Holy Scriptures, and in the writings and traditions of the early Church. We promise to honor them and consult them as our primary guide to following the Way of Jesus Christ. These same apostles also, facing remarkable odds, maintained a fellowship—through changes in doctrine over the inclusion of Gentiles, changes in leadership, pressure from synagogue leaders and civil authorities. We are called to maintain that fellowship, more strongly bonded even than the Company of the Ring, to stay in community with one another no matter our disagreements. The apostle Paul teaches that all Christians, by virtue of our baptism, are part of the Body of Christ. The body works together, not separately. While "spiritual but not religious" might sound cool, given some of the problems found in organized religion (spoiler alert: the problem is us), a Christian is found in fellowship with other Christians. We promise that. We also promise to regularly follow Christ's command to break the bread in remembrance of him through the Eucharist, and to be faithful in prayer for one another, the world, and ourselves.

Persevere in resisting evil, and whenever you fall into sin, repent and return to the Lord.

The most important word in that sentence is "whenever." We promise to do our best to follow in the Way of Jesus Christ as outlined in the Holy Scriptures, interpreted in communion with other Christians, past and present, and in line with our human reason. But we know that it is in our nature to fail at this project. Humans tend toward pride and selfishness. We can't help it. And so when we inevitably fail to live up to the standards of perfection to which Christ calls us, we are called to acknowledge our failure, attempt to make amends, and wake up, ready to try again. It does no good to wallow in guilt, or to pretend that our sin was not a sin. Instead, we promise to humbly repent, and keep trying for the rest of our lives.

Proclaim by word and example the Good News of God in Christ.

"But God proves his love for us in that while we still were sinners Christ died for us."[2] Despite the inevitability of our sin, the Good News is that God loved us enough to die for us. And all he asks in return is for us to love one another as he loved us. Part of that love is sharing the Good News. Unfortunately, some Christians have overused the "word" type of evangelizing and underused the "example" type. Running people down and yelling at them how sinful they are is (a) not super effective and (b) not exactly following Jesus's example of loving folks no matter what they believed and no matter how they lived. But some Christians have gone the other direction entirely, and kept the Good News of God in Christ secret, as though they were slightly embarrassed by Jesus. That's not the right way either. If you're on this journey, you've got to bring balance to the Force here, not pretend it doesn't exist.

Seek and serve Christ in all persons, loving your neighbor as yourself.

Man, these commitments just keep getting tougher. Not only are we asked to love our neighbors as ourselves, we are asked to seek out the Christ that exists in all of us, even the most annoying, selfish, or cruel, and to serve the Christ in that person. So let's parse this out. When the Son of God became human in the person of Jesus Christ, by uniting divinity to a human body, he enabled all human beings to carry the weight of divinity. The early Church called this *divinization*, the process of becoming divine. Cool, right? The hitch is, that divinization is happening for everyone, even if they don't recognize it. So some folks might not be in a place where they want to recognize the divine in their neighbors, and might treat them cruelly. Those people still carry some Christ within them, and we are called to seek that Christ out and serve it, no matter whether those persons respond with kindness. Liberation theologian Howard Thurman calls this the "Love-ethic" that is central to the religion of Jesus. "Every[one] is potentially every other [person's] neighbor."[3]

Strive for justice and peace among all people, and respect the dignity of every human being.

Once again, this commitment applies to all people, and every human being; even those who do not respect our dignity. We have been asked to assist God, the Creator of the Universe, in making manifest the kingdom of heaven, and in the kingdom of heaven, there is justice and peace between all people. Peace does not mean the absence of conflict, but rather the presence of harmony. The prophet Micah says that "they shall all sit under their own vines and under their own fig trees, and no one shall make them afraid";[4] (they'll be safe in the nation we've made.)[5] This means that in the kingdom of heaven, everyone has the resources they need to not jealously guard what they have. In order for there to be peace, there must be justice and respect first.

All right. Now that we've got the big commitments out of the way, we are ready to begin our quest. But first, we need to orient ourselves to this new Player's Handbook. Now, some geeks like to dive right in, learn by experience (spoiler alert: I am one of these), while others like to read the user's manual of every piece of equipment they buy. As an Episcopalian, I highly recommend the both/and. Seminary students use the phrase "both/and" to mean that a choice described as either/or does not really demand choosing one or the other. Read the outline here, and explore the prayer book on your own. Read through it cover to cover as though it were a novel, to orient yourself to all the treasures it contains. *And* dive right in by attending your local church. As you join the community in the rhythms of prayer, they will eventually feel familiar to you. You will be able to participate in traditions older, larger, deeper, and more communal than just yourself.

The Player's Handbook
A Rudimentary Guide to the Book of Common Prayer

In which we study the adventure path

[Prayer book n00bs start here. We will orient you to this all-important Player's Handbook for your life in the church. Level 30s skip to "The Adventure Path" on page 89.]

Entire thousand-page books have been written on the history of the Book of Common Prayer, so believe me when I say this is *brief*. It provides important context for the prayer book we have today. But if history ain't your bag, skip down to find an intro to today's prayer book on page 25.

A History of the Book(s) of Common Prayer

The first Book of Common Prayer (BCP) was written mostly by Thomas Cranmer, then archbishop of Canterbury, in 1549 (he had a council of advisors, but come on). This prayer book was based predominantly on the Sarum rite, which was an approved rite for use in the region of Salisbury (which was called Sarum in Latin) (The More You Know™).[1] The first BCP was the culmination of decades of work to convince King Henry VIII (he of the many wives) to allow the worship of God in English. Henry did allow translation of the Bible and the writing of a Great Litany, but it wasn't until after his death that we actually see the creation of the first English Book of Common Prayer.

Being a Reformation text, this BCP was very different from what you'd see in an Episcopal Church today. There was a great deal of anti-Catholic panic. Candles on the altar, even calling it an altar instead of a table—totally taboo. God forbid any of words in the Eucharistic Prayer suggest that something might be happening to the bread and the wine [Need to know now? Turn to "Magic" on page 119]. The 1549 Book of Common Prayer threads a very fine needle as it tries to keep on board folks who fear change, and keep those seeking greater reform from running off to the Lutherans or Presbyterians (it didn't totally work, but at least allowed the Church of England to exist as a separate entity with a theology of its own). We see this change with the 1552 prayer book, which goes farther than the incremental steps taken in the 1549. We quit calling the Eucharist "Mass," and got rid of the word "altar" entirely. The iconoclasm had begun—think Kylo Ren throwing a giant tantrum and lightsabering a technological panel to death, only instead of a lightsaber we have more . . . traditional weapons, and instead of a technological panel, we've got any artist's depiction of any Bible character or saint ever. You can still see the scars in England's churches. Canterbury Cathedral lost its shrine to St. Thomas à Becket, who had to go not only because he was a miracle-dispensing saint (heresy), but also because he had advocated for the power of the Roman Catholic Church over the monarchy, and Henry's followers couldn't possibly allow that.

Time for a dance break—if by "dance" you mean, "dance in the fires of Bloody Mary." Queen Mary I comes in, restores the Roman Catholic worship, burns heretics at the stake, and then dies in 1558 with no heir. Cranmer himself was put to the flame, after three years of torture and imprisonment. When Queen Elizabeth was swept onto the throne in 1559, it was time for yet another prayer book. You'll actually see this up until 1662; every time a new monarch ascends to the throne, they have to rewrite the book (not least because they need a reprint anyway, with the new monarch's name to pray for).

So what happened in 1662? The English Civil War happened. Decades of strife and violence, regicide, and Cromwell's rule had devastated the church. The politics of putting together a new prayer book were tricky. After all, in England, certain liturgical and theological practices were associated with the monarchy, and others with the Lord Protector. There were no simple proposals. Every word, every phrase, every prayer was associated with all kinds of baggage. Take kneeling while receiving communion. Seems simple enough, right? Wrong. There were many for whom kneeling to receive the bread and wine meant allegiance to the doctrine of Transubstantiation, which for them was completely unacceptable.

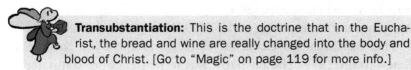

Transubstantiation: This is the doctrine that in the Eucharist, the bread and wine are really changed into the body and blood of Christ. [Go to "Magic" on page 119 for more info.]

But for others, not kneeling to receive communion was irreverent, arrogant, and faithless. What to do? They re-instituted the very flashy-sounding "Black Rubric," which clarified that kneeling whilst receiving communion did not imply adoration of the corporal Body of Christ, which was off in heaven, thank you very much.

I wish it were as cool as it sounds, but the **Black Rubric** is just a reference to the fact that in early prayer books most of the *rubrics* (directions) were printed in red, and this one was printed in black, probably because it was added at the last minute to avoid debates about it.

This process was so political that the English have never managed to update their prayer book since. If you worship in England today, you'll see that the Book of Common Prayer remains that which was published in 1662. It requires an Act of Parliament to change, and after hundreds of years and several attempts (the last in 1928), the Church of England appears to have resigned itself to the fact that it won't. Instead, they went outside the law to write a new masterwork, Common Worship 2000. Common Worship isn't one book, but rather a series of books, with a huge variety of prayers for many occasions. Most of it is available for free online, so check it out.

Episcopalians, however, have a completely different history. We used the 1662 like everybody else when the first priests came over to serve the thirteen colonies. But following the American Revolution, we had to make a change. No more prayers for the king, for example. So we got a new book in 1789. This book made no major theological or liturgical innovations, by design. The preface even declared that intention, saying, "this Church is far from intending to depart from the Church of England in any essential point of doctrine, discipline, or worship; or further than local circumstances require."[2] Being a disestablished church that had no part of the state, we revised it whenever we felt it necessary. The liturgical changes were minor until the writing of the 1979 Book of Common Prayer.

That Baptismal Covenant we talked about in the last chapter? All new to the 1979. The Eucharist was re-written, or re-translated from earlier sources, with a new emphasis on the Incarnation of Jesus, rather than the Crucifixion. We stopped referring to God as "thee" and "thou."[3] These and other changes shocked and alienated many, and led to a backlash against the new prayer book. There are still some churches today, in the Year of Our Lord 2017, that use the Book of Common Prayer 1928 for their regular worship, though most bishops discourage that practice.

For n00bs, the Book of Common Prayer 1979 (or whatever is in common use in your country and local church) is completely adequate as a Player's Handbook. It contains all you need to be able to build your character as a follower of Jesus in the Anglican Way. But as you geek out more on the intricacies of Anglican worship, there are hundreds of books for you to study. Nearly every province has written its own, sometimes several. Popular prayer books include the most recent ones from Ireland and New Zealand. I am personally a big fan of *Our Modern Services,* a new-ish eucharistic rite from the Anglican Church of Kenya. But first, take a look at the Book of Common Prayer 1979. Read, mark, learn, and inwardly digest it. For an Episcopalian, it is the source of all theology and practice—sometimes even over and above the Bible. You might hear us say how nice it is that Scripture quotes the prayer book so often. Take a look, it's in [the] book![4]

You've probably heard the church described variously as "Episcopal" and "Anglican." What do those two words mean, and is there a difference between them? **Episcopal** (see more on page 39) means "ruled by bishops" and could theoretically apply to any of the many churches that have bishops in leadership positions. It usually only applies, though, to those churches in the **Anglican** tradition. These churches have a heritage that goes back to the Church of England. Churches in communion with the See (archbishop) of Canterbury are part of what's known as the **Anglican Communion** (jump to *Let's break it down* on page 116 for a full explanation), and may describe themselves as either Episcopal or Anglican. The Episcopal Church is a part of the Anglican Communion, but does not usually refer to itself as Anglican, though it may refer to certain things it does as Anglican. It's confusing. Just nod along.

Understanding the Prayer Book

Let's start at the very be-ginning . . .[5]

Seriously, though, page 1 is a great place to start. The Book of Common Prayer 1979 begins with the Ratification and the Preface from the 1789 edition. They lay out the purpose behind writing a prayer book at all:

> The particular Forms of Divine Worship, and the Rites and Ceremonies appointed to be used therein, being things in their own

nature indifferent, and alterable, and so acknowledged; it is but reasonable that upon weighty and important considerations, according to the various exigency of times and occasions, such changes and alterations should be made therein, as to those that are in place of Authority should, from time to time, seem either necessary or expedient.

Translation: Any prayers can praise God, but it is useful for us all to pray together; this is why the United States needed a new one post-Revolution (spoiler alert: clergy could no longer swear an oath of loyalty to the king); an explainer that our Book is a companion to, not a departure from, the Book of Common Prayer of the Church of England.

Next, we have "Concerning the Service of the Church." This should be considered your foundation—at least as far as community worship is concerned. It lays out the basic framework through which we should view the worship of the Church as Episcopalians understand it. The Holy Eucharist, Morning Prayer, and Evening Prayer are listed as the primary worship services for Episcopalians. It's actually great; instead of the party having to fight over who's front line and who are the casters in the back, this section lays out for you who goes where and who does what. There are a couple options, depending on your context (and at the discretion of the bishop), but it lays out the basics for you.

The Calendar of the Church Year

Episcopalians don't mess around when it comes to ordering our calendar. Everything is based on the two biggest feasts of the year: Christmas and Easter. You know those, right? Christmas: when Jesus is born, every year on December 25, Mary, Joseph, some animals, some shepherds, that whole thing. Easter: Jesus is resurrected after dying on a cross, moveable feast, pastel colors, symbols of new life, bunnies, eggs, all that. But there's way more to it than that.

Every day of the year is part of a season. The church year begins with **Advent.** Advent begins every year four Sundays before

Christmas, usually immediately after Thanksgiving. It's a time of celebration, of anticipation, of preparing the Way for Jesus to come—both as a baby born to Mary of Nazareth, and in the Second Coming with Phenomenal, Cosmic Powers™. Next we celebrate that coming in the season of **Christmas.** The twelve days of Christmas start *on* December 25. What if, instead of ceasing to listen to Christmas music immediately after Christmas Day, we only started listening to it then, and didn't stop until January 6, the day of **Epiphany**?

Epiphany commemorates the coming of the Wise Men, and the revealing to all humankind the mystery of Christ made Incarnate as a human being. This season can last a long or a short time, depending on the day of Easter, and its biggest celebration is the **Baptism of Our Lord**.

Easter Day moves around to correspond to the date of Passover, which is based on the lunar calendar. There are all sorts of complicated tables in the back of the prayer book to help you determine when it is, but now that Google exists, you're better off trusting the Cylons with the task of determining this information.

Then it's time for **Lent.** Lent is the biggie. It is The Season. It's the shindig. The Gathering. The time when even those who haven't darkened the door of a church for a year are seen walking around with ash crosses on their foreheads. Which is strange, because it's also the saddest: the time when we remember our mortality, and our sinfulness, our need to repent from our evil ways, and our utter inability to do so. Why this appeals to the masses I'll never understand, but as a clergyperson, I'm grateful.

Lent culminates in **Holy Week**, the time when we remember Jesus's last week: cleansing the Temple, being anointed at Bethany, washing his disciples' feet, and carrying his cross to Golgotha. Holy Week includes Holy Saturday, when we remember Jesus hanging out in the tomb (and harrowing hell, which is just the coolest doctrine ever), which concludes at sundown on Saturday with **Easter.**

Most churches celebrate Easter on Sunday morning, which makes sense, given that all four Gospels have a human being first encounter Jesus at dawn, but Episcopalians jump right in at the very first possible moment (Jewish days, as you may know, begin at sundown the night before—hence, why Shabbat services are on Friday nights. So if Jesus was raised on Sunday, we can celebrate it beginning on sundown at Saturday). We celebrate Easter for fifty days.

> The **Harrowing of Hell** is the belief that while Jesus was dead, he went down to hell to rescue everyone there. This is not an event described in Scripture—Jesus doesn't resurrect and then tell his disciples all about his adventures in hell—but the Church believed from the very beginning that Christ, as the Second Adam, rescued Adam and Eve and triumphed over the Death they had introduced into the world.

Forty days in, we remember Jesus's **Ascension**, and the season culminates with **Pentecost**, when we remember the coming of the Holy Spirit to Jesus's disciples. After Pentecost, we enter **Ordinary Time**, the longest season, which the Godly Play[6] community calls "the great, green, growing Sundays of the year" and the rest of us call "spend the majority of your vestment budget on the green stuff because we have to look at it for six months."

Within each season are days that are special, and this section tells us how to prioritize those. Some days are what's called "fixed" (which means they occur on a particular day); Christmas, for example, is always on December 25. Epiphany is always on January 6. The Presentation is always February 2. Other days are "moveable feasts." Easter we've already discussed. Pentecost is always fifty days after Easter. Palm Sunday falls exactly one week before. You get the picture. Well, moving some feasts and not others means sometimes there's a conflict. So we need a guide to help us prioritize. You know how in the Player's Handbook it'll say, "This spell doesn't stack with Haste"? It's like that. Some feasts, especially those commemorating events in the life of Christ, always take priority.

The Daily Office

Now that we've spent a dragon's age talking about the ins and outs of the calendar, we come to **the Daily Office**. Like many faiths, we have a tradition of praying several times a day, at particular times. Jews pray morning, noon, and evening. Muslims pray before sunrise, shortly after noon, mid-afternoon, after sunset, and before bed. And Episcopalians pray in the morning, at noon, at sundown, and before bed. These prayers are known as **Morning Prayer, Noonday Prayer, Evening Prayer,** and **Compline.** Anyone can pray these prayers—alone or in a large group, the whole office or just one service per day—or even per week. You don't need a priest to be present. They contain multitudes: prayers of confession and assurance of absolution, songs and poems from Scripture and tradition, intercession for the community, and the heart of the office, the Psalms. The Psalms are the prayer book of the Bible, our only record of what the ancient Israelites said to our God over three thousand years ago. And in each office of the day, our longest piece is always from the Psalms, connecting us with our ancient heritage.

For whatever reason, one of the treasures of the Anglican tradition is that of Evensong. Over the last five hundred years and more, our English forebears developed a tradition of a choir singing the evening office. There are special *canticles* (poems from Scripture) appointed for the evening, especially the *Magnificat*, Mary's song of joy at the news of her pregnancy with Jesus, and the *Nunc dimittis*, Simeon's song of satisfaction that he had seen the Savior born and presented in the Temple. Hundreds of composers have written settings for these canticles, for the prayers, for the entire service. Some of these sound like they belong in *The Tudors*, others are extremely contemporary. If you want to hear choir kids nerd out, ask them about their favorite Evensong settings. And if you want to hear some of the most beautiful music ever sung, go to Evensong in an English cathedral.

If the offices (which usually take between ten and forty-five minutes) are too long for you, you can try the **Daily Devotions for**

Individuals and Families. These one-page services are designed for families who seek guidance as they pray together, and for busy individuals who want a place to anchor their daily prayers so that they don't get stuck only praying what I like to call Cosmic Butler™ prayers: prayers that assume God is some kind of all-powerful servant, just waiting to accede to all our petty requests. "Please help me catch that light, punish the guy who cut me off, let my favorite team make the playoffs, may the cute girl message me on OKCupid." God is not the *Star Trek* computer. And praying the Daily Devotions reminds us to pray not only for our needs and for those we know who are suffering, but also to give thanks, to offer praise and adoration, and to confess our sins and seek forgiveness. But it's nice to have a lightning round option for days when you might be in a hurry.

Why do we call the last prayer of the day **Compline** instead of Night Prayer or Last Prayer or Bedtime Prayer? The word "Compline" is English, really—it comes from the Latin *completorium*, which is the same word that gives us the word *complete*. Compline completes the day; it signifies that our work and worship are finished. In a monastery, Compline signifies the beginning of the Great Silence, which is kept until the first office of the new day.

Special Days, Special Prayers

For days when you're looking for a more, shall we say, comprehensive prayer, there follows **the Great Litany.** Written to be chanted in procession, the Great Litany was the first liturgy translated into English. When you pray it, you are participating in the most ancient English way of praying. The Great Litany is a *call and response* prayer, wherein a leader bids prayers for deliverance from various specific ills. A Fillorian litany might go, "From giants, from foxes, from giant rams, from our own inadequacy and self-loathing, Good Lord, deliver us."[7]

But if you're praying the Great Litany at different times of the year, you need prayers to match those different times. These prayers are called the **Collects**, because they collect the prayers of the people into a summary of the theme of the day. Collects for a holy day or a saint tell you something about that day or that saint. Collects for a Sunday offer prayers appropriate for the season (for example in Lent we pray for forgiveness, in Easter we give thanks for grace of salvation) that might match the readings. The Collect directs and focuses our prayers and reminds us what our prayers that day are for. They keep us from always praying the exact same thing.

Proper Liturgies for Special Days come next. These *orders of service* are for one-time services that are so dramatic, so strange, so different from our usual way of worshiping they need their own liturgies to properly remember these events in the life of Jesus. **Ash Wednesday** is not something Jesus celebrated, but it invites us to the observance of a holy Lent, that season of fasting, repentance, and self-examination wherein we remember Jesus's Passion—his sacrifice of his life for ours. You may have seen the trendy **Ashes To Go** folks around your town on a Wednesday in February or early March. They are encouraging you to observe a holy Lent. They are offering you the chance to remember your mortality. "All we go down to the dust. . . ." While this may not be the most pleasant reality check, it is a chance to remember to live your life more meaningfully, more intentionally. It is a reminder that even the most righteous and godly of us will die, and that even the most sinful and evil of us has a chance to repent.

After five weeks of Lent, we come to **Holy Week**, commemorated with the remainder of these special liturgies. On **Palm Sunday**, we make great procession with palms to welcome our King. It looks not unlike the Yunkish slaves welcoming Daenerys to Yunkai with their calls of "Mhysa."[8] But by the end of the worship, we have begun to read the **Passion Gospel**, a dramatic retelling of Jesus's arrest, trial, and crucifixion. In some churches, they chant this incredibly long Scripture reading, apparently under the theory that merely having to stand for the entire story is penance enough, but most churches read it through, with the congregation playing the part of the crowd. This powerful ritual reminds us that we are not better than our ancestors who called to be given Barabbas (a murderer) rather than Jesus. As a dear friend of mine says, "Everyone wants to believe that if they had been in Germany in the 1930s, they wouldn't have been a Nazi. But a lot of people were Nazis." All of us have the capacity to sacrifice human life to maintain the status quo, the capacity to trample over others on our way to the top, or, more likely, to keep the spot we have. The reading of the **Passion Gospel** reminds us that it is not just the KKK and other hate groups that are sinners and the rest of us are righteous—that we all participate in crucifying those most like Jesus in our own day.

This Gospel is so important that we will read it again, in the exact same way, on **Good Friday.** But first, we have **Maundy Thursday**, a feast of remembrance of the New Commandment (in Latin, *mandatum novum*) Jesus gives us: to love one another, to express that love through humble service (such as a foot washing), and to remember him in the breaking of bread and the sharing of the cup. Just as we remember his triumphant entry to Jerusalem with a procession of palms, we celebrate this memory with a re-enactment of his example of servant leadership, by inviting the congregation forward to have their feet washed. The worship concludes with the Stripping of (no, not on) the Altar. The clergy solemnly remove all linens, vessels, and any remaining finery from the sanctuary.

Communion bread after it's been consecrated is called the **Host**. To me, that always conjures images of Jesus, the host of this banquet, but apparently it comes from the Latin for "sacrificial victim" and has nothing to do with hospitality at all.

The consecrated Host is removed to a special place, usually decorated as a garden, where the people are invited to observe **the Watch.** The concept of the Watch is best explained (IMHO) by Diana Gabaldon at the end of *Outlander*, in the person of Brother Anselm. "You recall the Bible, and the story of Gethsemane, where

Our Lord waited out the hours before His trial and crucifixion, and His friends, who should have borne Him company, all fell fast asleep?" The Watch is our opportunity to wait one hour in the garden with him, to adore him, to thank him, or just to simply be. Anselm continues, when asked what he does in that hour, "I sit, and I look at Him. . . . And He looks at me."[9]

The proper liturgies conclude with the **Easter Vigil**, the pinnacle of the church year, the hub that holds the spokes of the wheel around which all our Christian life circles. We begin at sundown, in darkness, with the kindling of the new fire. We call the heavenly host and choirs of angels to rejoice with us on this holy night in the ancient song of the *Exultet*. We recall the history of salvation, beginning with God's Creation of the world, and the promise that all people would gather on God's holy mountain. We welcome new members of the Body of Christ in baptism, and renew our own baptismal promises. And we celebrate the First Eucharist of Easter with the peal of bells and calls of "Alleluia!" as the church is filled with a blaze of light.

Sacraments and Rites

The **Easter Vigil** celebrates both of the major *dominical* (that is, coming directly from Our Lord) sacraments, which are the next sections of the Book of Common Prayer, **Holy Baptism** and **Holy Eucharist.** Holy Baptism is the door (that is, the metaphorical door) by which we enter the Christian community. It's usually not quite so dramatic as Delmar's impromptu baptism in *O Brother, Where Art Thou?*, and certainly never so thorough as to require resuscitation—we do not follow the Drowned God. But in baptism we are buried with Christ, and as we rise from the water we are raised with him in resurrection. We die to sin and are raised a new creation. The dividing wall between us is broken down, and we become co-inheritors with Christ of all God's promises. The Episcopal Church baptizes all comers; anyone from the moment they emerge from the womb to the moment they take their last breath may be baptized. In the Book of Acts, the Ethiopian eunuch said, "Here is water, what doth hinder me from being baptized?"[10] We have answered: nothing.

If **Baptism** is the door by which we enter the Body of Christ, then the **Holy Eucharist** is the meal that sustains and feeds that Body on its earthly pilgrimage. The prayer book contains two rites, an order, and eight eucharistic prayers, so no matter your liturgical proclivities you can find a Eucharist for you. Most primary Sunday services at most Episcopal churches are Rite II, but here and there (like at my church) you can find one that prays according to Rite I. The most obvious difference between them is the language. Rite I retains the "thee/thou/thine" language typical of Archbishop Cranmer's day, while Rite II keeps the prayers mostly the same, but updates the language to match our more typical way of speaking today. They represent two different philosophies of worship: the "Sunday best" idea, and the "Come as you are" idea. The "Sunday best" philosophy believes that we ought to offer to God our best—nice clothes, elevated language—to honor God by setting apart the time we spend with him as special and different. The "Come as you are" way of being encourages us to rest in the idea that we are already accepted and loved by God just as we are, and that we needn't—shouldn't—change anything about ourselves, for worship is part of our daily life and our whole being. Both of these are fine ways of thinking; as a variety junkie, I go from one to the other fairly regularly. Some feel very strongly about one way of worshipping over the other. Episcopalians, as true geeks, love to argue about liturgy. But God is praised either way—ultimately, it's a matter of personal preference.

After the dominical sacraments, we come to the **Pastoral Offices**. These are a series of rites of passage, listed roughly in the order most people go through them. Their place in Episcopal liturgy is somewhat uncertain; some Episcopalians class many of them as *sacraments* as our Roman Catholic cousins do. They may not be *dominical*, as in, Jesus never explicitly commanded us to do them, but the Church has historically witnessed them as "outward and visible signs of inward and spiritual grace," as one of our greatest theologians has said. Others say that as their origin lies outside of Scripture, they are more properly called *sacramental rites* or *offices*.

I know it's not very geek-like of me to declare that I have no dog in this fight, but I honestly couldn't care less. To me, the main difference between the dominical sacraments and these rites (beyond the fact that Jesus didn't directly command us to do them) is that not everyone needs to do all of them. Not everyone needs to get married. Not everyone needs to make private confession. Not everyone needs to be ordained. Episcopalians have a saying, "All may, some should, none must." But everyone does need to get baptized. Everyone needs to receive communion, preferably as often as possible. These sacraments make present to us "the innumerable benefits procured unto us"[11] by Jesus's life, death, and resurrection. The others are much more optional.

The first Pastoral Office is **Confirmation.** This somewhat incoherent rite rises from the early days of the church, when only bishops could baptize. As the church grew, this became geographically impractical, and they deputized priests to manage the dipping (that's the literal translation of the Greek word βαπτιζω, *baptizo*) of babies. They reserved to themselves the *chrismation,* or anointing with oil, though. So it often happened that new Christians were baptized, and then confirmed whenever the bishop made it to that town.

Nowadays, Confirmation is more of an adult affirmation of faith: an Oath-Taking, a declaration of allegiance, an acceptance of vows made on one's behalf in infancy. Think of it like royalty. The crown prince (or princess) is named at birth, and the reigning monarch commits to raising this child in preparation for their eventual rule. But it is not until adolescence when the child recognizes his or her own responsibility for the kingdom that they make their own commitment to a lifetime of service. The next office is just that: **A Form of Commitment to Christian Service.** It's a chance for the party to gather before heading off on their quest, to ask the Deity to bless their endeavors, as they promise to be faithful and true.

A nerdy note: Many Episcopalians, perhaps unsurprisingly, are *Anglophiles*. Since our cultural heritage is primarily English, and our traditions are steeped in the tea of British peculiarity, many of us find ourselves irresistibly drawn to British-isms. In addition, Queen Elizabeth II is the Supreme Governor of the Church of England. Many of our particular cultural traditions come from a close connection with the royal family. The royal wedding was perhaps the most watched Anglican worship service in recent history. So you'll often hear Episcopalians express an irrational fondness for royal-isms.

The next office is one that is definitely optional, but many Christians seem to have opted in. **The Celebration and Blessing of a Marriage** is perhaps the most commonly used of these rites, though there are others listed. The marriage rite has remained largely unchanged since the first Book of Common Prayer in 1549. "Mawwidge is wut bwings us togevver today"[12]—whoops, I totally mean, "Dearly beloved: We have come together in the presence of God to witness and bless the joining together of this man and this woman in Holy Matrimony."[13] The opening preamble lays it all out for us: The purpose of marriage is mutual joy, help, and comfort in prosperity and adversity; and, when it is God's will, for the procreation of children. Procreation is not the only or even the primary reason for marriage, but for those couples choosing to have kids, marriage is designed to help with that project. In weddings, as in most others of these rites, we make vows. We don't write our own (usually), but we join in the great tradition of those who have made these exact same vows for hundreds of years. We pray for the couple, that their lives might reflect God's love to the world. And we share the peace of Christ with them as the priest pronounces them husband and wife—no "you may kiss the bride" here!

After the marriage rite, we have an office for **Thanksgiving for the Birth or Adoption of a Child.** This too-rarely used office is derived from the traditional practice known as the **Churching of Women.** That practice followed the laws laid down in Leviticus for the purification of women after childbirth—the idea being that a woman should avoid attending church prior to partaking in this rite. As society began to reject the idea that women were ritually impure during menstruation and following childbirth (and about time), the rite changed to emphasize thanksgiving to God for the woman's safety through the sometimes harrowing delivery of her child. The current version involves both parents and the whole congregation and emphasizes thanksgiving for the gift of the child, and the welcome of the child into the community. Childbirth is a lot scarier of a biological process than we tend to admit, and offering thanksgiving for preservation through it, not to mention the gift of new life in the form of a healthy child, is worth taking the time to do. It has no effect on one's purity, though.

Is marriage only between a man and a woman? Actually, no. The *canons* (that would be rules not relating to liturgy) were changed at the 78th General Convention in 2015 to say that the official Episcopal teaching regarding marriage is: "that God's purpose for our marriage is for our mutual joy, for the help and comfort we will give to each other in prosperity and adversity, and, when it is God's will, for the gift and heritage of children and their nurture in the knowledge and love of God. We also understand that our marriage is to be unconditional, mutual, exclusive, faithful, and lifelong; and *we engage to make the utmost effort to accept these gifts and fulfill these duties, with the help of God and the support of our community.*"[14] We have written extra prayer book resources to celebrate and bless marriages between persons of the same sex. The Book of Common Prayer is part of our Constitution, and as such is extraordinarily difficult to change. Not only does it take two consecutive General Conventions to do so, once you open the door to change a little, everybody wants to change a lot. So folks get antsy about changing anything. This means that it will be some time (though hopefully not much) before this opening preamble is changed. In short: Marriage between any two persons (at least one person must be baptized) is allowed in the Episcopal Church, but any clergyperson may decline to solemnize any marriage, and some clergy are required by their bishops to decline to solemnize marriages between persons of the same sex.

After one gets married and has a kid, what happens next? We sin. Or at least, my friends who are parents tell me they're made much more aware of their sin. So we have the opportunity to confess that sin and receive assurance of absolution in the **Reconciliation of a Penitent.** Many, or even most, Episcopalians opt not to practice this rite—we need no intermediary between God and us, after all. But there is something freeing about telling all the worst things about yourself to another human, one you can see, having them assure you that God forgives you, and then saying no more about it afterward. In our general confession we say that "the burden of [our sins] is intolerable"[15] and in the rite of Reconciliation we can physically feel that burden being lifted. At least, I can. Instead of feeling as though I'm totally out of whack, completely beyond the pale, I can feel like I'm . . . normal. Human. Flawed, but not in such a way that horrifies my confessor. It's comforting. YMMV.

So now we're confirmed, married, be-parented, and shriven (that's from the Old English and means one who has confessed and been absolved), we might get sick. And we have a rite for that. Commonly known as *Last Rites* and dramatically portrayed in the movies, **Ministration to the Sick** and **Ministration at the Time of Death** are decidedly less exciting than they appear on TV. Lightning does not come out of my hands like Emperor Palpatine when I anoint someone with oil, nor do people throw off their walkers or leap out of their wheelchairs.

> **The Letter of James** is basically a collection of practical advice for Christian living, interspersed with harsh judgments on those whom James thinks are Doing It Wrong, namely people who show favoritism and rich people who exploit their workers. At the end though, he gives some quick tips, including the gem that anyone who is sick should call the elders to pray and anoint them with oil.

Ministration to the Sick is more about healing than cure, more about holistic peace than quick fixes, more about thanking God for the good work of physicians than about subverting their important work with magic. Ministration to the Sick has three parts: Ministry of the Word, which includes Bible readings, prayers, and the opportunity to confess one's sins; Laying on of Hands and Anointing, which is commended to us in the Bible as a means of healing,[16] and Holy Communion. Either of the first two parts can be done independently; Holy Communion ought really to be done in conjunction with the Ministry of the Word. It's hard to receive the Sacrament without first hearing the Gospel.

Ministration at the Time of Death is really no different, except that it recognizes the inevitability of the person's death, and commends their soul to God for safekeeping, rather than expressing a desire for recovery. It concludes with a rite for the **Reception of a Body**, which begins the rite of the **Burial of the Dead**. We receive the body of the deceased at the church; pray for the soul of the departed, that they might grow in the knowledge and love of God, and enter into the land of light and joy in the communion of all God's saints; celebrate the Holy Eucharist, our means of joining in the heavenly banquet together with all those who have gone before us; and commit their body to the ground. As you might suspect, the Burial Office is the last rite of passage we go through, and the last Pastoral Office in the prayer book.

Episcopal Services

Next we have the **Episcopal Services.** Wait, what? We're all Episcopalian, it's an Episcopal prayer book, aren't all the services

So the word *Episcopal* comes from the Greek word *episkopos* which means overseer, supervisor, or ruler. The early church used this word, which would eventually be translated into English as "bishop," to describe the folks who led the Church. So we're called the Episcopal Church because we are a church that is led by bishops, and Episcopal Services are services that must be conducted or presided over by bishops.

Episcopal? Well, like most things, it depends. Episcopal Services are those services that must be conducted by bishops. But already we are in difficulties; **Confirmation** (remember, the first of the **Pastoral Offices**) is to be performed by a bishop as well. Let's skip past that, though.

The bulk of this section is made up of the **Ordination Rites**, the services by which we make new bishops, priests, and deacons. Bishops, as we will discuss in the next chapter, are the supervisors, the leaders of the church. A **bishop** presides over and administrates a diocese. She guards the faith, unity, and discipline of the Church, she ordains new priests and deacons to fulfill their role in ministry in Christ's holy catholic Church. Together with other bishops, she shares in the leadership of the Church throughout the world. She boldly proclaims and interprets the Gospel of Christ, nourishes the gifts of all baptized people from the riches of God's grace, and is merciful to all, shows compassion to the poor and strangers, and defends those who have no helper.

It takes three bishops to make a bishop in our tradition, although legend has it that as St. Brigid was being ordained abbess of Kildare, the bishop presiding accidentally said the words to make a bishop instead of an abbess (this was around 480, so a minute or two before we started ordaining women to the episcopate). Many of those present called for a do-over, but the bishop followed the example of Pontius Pilate and said, basically, "What I have written, I have written." So she stayed a bishop. (No joke, a friend of mine was ordained deacon on the Feast of St. Brigid and was accidentally ordained a bishop as well. St. Brigid and God have a wicked sense of humor. Her bishop went back and redid the ordination right, though.)

Priests are called to a different job than bishops, and are subordinate to them. That's actually one of the first questions they ask you in the service of the **Ordination of a Priest**. "Will you respect and be guided by the pastoral direction and leadership of your bishop?" Priests proclaim by word and deed the Gospel of Jesus Christ (the bishop does the job of interpreting), they love and serve the people among whom they work, caring alike for young and old, strong and weak, rich and poor. They preach, declare God's forgiveness to penitent sinners, pronounce God's blessing, and share (with bishops—those guys have their fingers in every pie) in the administration of Holy Baptism, and in the celebration of the mysteries of Christ's body and blood. Priests, then, are the workers overseen by the *episkopoi*, the supervisors.

Also overseen by the bishops are deacons. The **Ordination of a Deacon** lays out the servant ministry of the deacons (the word "deacon" comes from the Greek *diakonos*, or servant). Deacons are the workers who are sent out to interpret to the Church the needs, concerns, and hopes of the world. Their ministry is particularly to those on the margins of society—the poor, the weak, the sick, and the lonely. The first deacons were ordained in Jerusalem as described in the Acts of the Apostles, chapter 6, verse 1: "Now during those days, when the disciples were increasing in number, the Hellenists complained against the Hebrews because their widows were being neglected in the daily distribution of food." Basically, the racial group (Hellenists) that was considered lesser in the first Christian community needed help ensuring that their poorest and weakest citizens received their fair share in the charitable distributions of the community. The apostles chose seven believers to see to this task, the first deacons. The first among them, Stephen, was shortly thereafter stoned to death, the first follower of Jesus to follow his example of being publicly executed for the things he was saying. Being a deacon is no joke.

The other Episcopal Services are **Celebration of a New Ministry** and **The Dedication and Consecration of a Church**, services that celebrate the welcoming of a new priest to preside over a congregation and celebrate a new building for a congregation to work in. These are fairly infrequently celebrated, given that most churches don't call a new leader terribly often, and we're not building too many churches these days.

That's the end of the rites and services section of the prayer book. But there're plenty of appendices still left to go. The Book of Common Prayer is intended to be *useful*. It doesn't just give us the forms of services. It builds out all that is needful for our life in Christ. Next up, we have the **Psalter**—that is, a copy of the Psalms from the Bible. They show us how the people Israel prayed at the time of King David. They exhibit a huge breadth of *types* of prayers—adoration, lament, petition, and dedication. When you pray the Daily Office, no matter which office you pray, the Psalms are at the heart of it. Therefore, we have printed the Psalms in their entirety in the prayer book. No need to go find a Bible (it's a unique translation anyway, so your NRSV won't exactly match what we have in the BCP).

What's the deal with all these different versions of the Bible? Why are some people so hot for the KJV, when others insist on the NRSV? First you need to understand is that all English Bibles are works in translation. The Old Testament was originally written in Hebrew (mostly, some passages in Daniel are in Aramaic), and the New Testament in Greek. Any Bible you read in English has been translated, which is to say that it has been interpreted. All translation requires the translator to choose the most appropriate word, given history and context. There is no such thing as a literal translation; it would be incomprehensible if there were; different grammar structures alone [steps down from soapbox]. So the KJV is the King James Version, the version authorized by King James of England and Scotland in 1611. Since then, we think we've written better translations, referencing more ancient manuscripts, with greater understanding of ancient contexts. The NRSV is the most accepted in scholarly circles. The Psalms in the Book of Common Prayer are a boutique, in-house translation from Hebrew manuscripts, using what we knew in the 1970s.

After the Psalms is a section of **Prayers and Thanksgivings** for various occasions not related to the seasons of the church year, saints being commemorated, or other liturgical situations. These prayers take the same form as the **Collects**, back much earlier in the book. If you need a prayer during election season (yes, Jesus), this is where you'll find it. There're also prayers for birthdays, for quiet confidence, for the poor and the oppressed, for church musicians and artists, for the good use of leisure, for families, for rain, for the future of the human race. These prayers can be quite primal, addressing our fear of the elements. They can also be ordinary and mundane, addressing things like the Supreme Court. There are a vast variety of circumstances for which to pray, and we've got prayers for all of them.

Next we come to the **Catechism.** In traditional question and answer form, the Catechism lays out a simple outline of the faith. It tells you what you've already picked up by praying the prayers in the Book. It tells you what we believe. It is followed by the **Historical Documents of the Church**, which has yet to be taken up by Thermians[17] (to my knowledge). These documents are those from our history that we consider the most important in defining who we are. They come from as early as 451, when the Council of Chalcedon made a definitive declaration about the dual nature of Christ, and as late as 1886, when councils of bishops in Chicago and Lambeth declared the four things that are most essential to the Christian heritage.

> The four essential things, more formally referred to as the **Chicago-Lambeth Quadrilateral**, are: the Bible, the Nicene Creed, the sacraments of baptism and Eucharist, and the historic episcopate.

If you've made it this far, good for you! Only the geekiest of us ever venture to the very back of the prayer book. The advent of Google has made the section of **Tables for Finding Holy Days** rather useless, but I suppose it's not fair to have asked the Standing Commission for Liturgy and Music to have predicted that back in the 1970s.

The very last section of the Book of Common Prayer is the **Lectionary**. This table lays out a comprehensive plan to read the vast majority of the Bible in worship over three years. In recent years, most of the Episcopal Church has joined several other churches in using the Revised Common Lectionary. This ecumenical document attempts to ensure that as many churches are reading the same Scripture as possible. Back in early 2016, Donald Trump went to Iowa in his campaign for the presidency, and worshipped in a Presbyterian church. The Scripture lessons focused on humility, and Trump wondered if perhaps they were specifically chosen and directed at him. Episcopalians, Lutherans, Methodists, and Catholics all laughed—we had heard those same lessons that day, and they were chosen long ago.

The RCL isn't beloved by all Episcopalians though. It prioritizes trying to get absolutely the most Scripture read possible, which means that some of the readings are unbelievably long. And they don't fit together quite as tightly as the shorter readings from the original prayer book lectionary did. They made a theme. They tied in with the Collect of the Day. They matched the season. So if your church isn't doing the same readings as everyone else, they're probably following the lectionary from the prayer book. There is also a **Daily Office Lectionary**, which tells you the readings for Morning and Evening Prayer each day, and is on a two-year schedule, just to be confusing.

So that's the Book of Common Prayer. Practically perfect prayers for every practical occasion. If you're going to make a character, you not only need to understand the rules, you've got to figure out what role God is calling you to play.

[Turn the page to start exploring the orders of ministry. Jump to "Magic," page 119, if you're more interested in the theology behind the Book of Common Prayer.]

Classes
The Orders of Ministry

In which laypeople, bishops, priests, and deacons play a role

In church we don't have *quite* as many classes as in *Dungeons & Dragons*. And we certainly don't have hybrid classes, though a thing called "bi-vocational ministry" exists. A class, or *order*, is one's vocation—a calling. In D&D you have your sorcerers, your rangers, your barbarians, but over the last two thousand years the church has whittled it down to four: laypersons (also called the baptized), deacons, priests, and bishops. A class is more than a profession. It's central to our identity, and our way of relating to God and to the rest of the church. We call these classes *orders*, and changing orders involves a ritual usually called ordination. Deacons, priests, and bishops are known collectively as the clergy.

Anyone may be called by God to serve in any order—male or female, gay or straight, black, white, Asian, indigenous American, Hispanic/Latinx—anyone. Baptism, the rite by which one enters the Body of Christ and becomes a Christian, is open to everyone. Some churches expect that the baptismal candidate (or at least their parents and godparents) be instructed before being baptized, but our Scriptures include stories of the unlikeliest of people asking for baptism with no preparation at all. As previously mentioned, in the Book of Acts, an Ethiopian eunuch asked the apostle Philip, "Here is water, what doth hinder me from being baptized?"[1] When Cornelius the Gentile centurion showed Peter that he and his household had received the gift of the Holy Spirit, Peter baptized them with water immediately.[2]

Ordination to the other three orders isn't like that. At all. Since deacons, priests, and bishops serve in lifelong leadership roles in the church ("you are a priest forever, according to the order of Melchizedek"),[3] there is an extensive vetting process. Some people are called to be deacons forever, some are called to be deacons first and then priests, and some priests are finally called (as expressed by the will of the people in an election) to be bishops. All of these orders are called "holy," which means set apart. A life lived in holy orders is a lifelong commitment to being set apart as a servant of God, and more importantly, a servant of the servants of God. A call to holy orders must be verified by multiple groups of people—your rector, a parish discernment group, the diocesan Commission on Ministry, the Standing Committee, and finally, the bishop.

No order is better than any other order; as in gaming, there are pros and cons to each one. But it must be said that the Episcopal Church has a sad history of what is called clericalism, a practice of valuing the clergy's opinion over that of the laity. Since clergy tend to have degrees in theology, there is a tendency to think of them as professional Christians. Since clergy tend to pray more visibly more often, there is a tendency to think of them as more educated, more holy—better connected to God than everyone else. Since clergy tend to serve full-time in congregations, there is a tendency to think of them as best equipped to make decisions about that congregation's future. Well, clergy do have theology degrees, they (hopefully) pray frequently, and they spend at *minimum* forty hours per week thinking about what's best for a congregation (or whatever context they are serving), and it's worth considering those things. But that does not mean that a layperson is less qualified than an ordained person to think, talk, and decide about matters theological, prayerful, and administrative.

If anything, clergy ought to be listening more to the voice of the laity, for a couple reasons:

1. Laypeople are the front-line fighters of the Christian party. Clergy are the casters—they hang back, "buffing" with encouragement and teaching, "detecting magic" by naming the Holy in everyday life, and "healing," by offering the sacramental presence of God when that everyday life gets rough. As such, clerics need to listen to the needs of the front-liners—they're the ones out there, getting roughed up by a sinful, broken world. They're the ones improvising when there's no real playbook for what happens next. They're the ones actually putting the Christian life into practice in a world that is fundamentally incompatible with the way that Christ asked us to live. If what clergy are offering isn't actually helping that project, they're not contributing to the party.

2. The Church, at its best, is what a priest friend calls a "downwardly mobile institution." While bishops are theoretically the decision-makers and leaders of the Church, having been elected to that office by the people they serve, at each stage of leadership, they pick up a heavier cross. It cannot be denied that Christian leaders have sometimes passed that cross along to a

convenient Simon of Cyrene figure, to make someone (or some group) carry it for them. This has happened most recently to LGBTQ+ Christians, but women, black people, indigenous groups around the New World, abuse victims, and others have had the cross shoved on them at one time or another. But carrying the cross of Jesus is meant to be first, a voluntary effort, and second, something done in the service of others, not as a club to beat them with.

Let's talk about classes in specific now:

The Laity

All baptized persons are ministers of the Church. As we discussed in the chapter on the Ultimate Quest (page 14), we all promise in the rite of baptism to follow the Baptismal Covenant. So our primary ministry is to:

- Continue in the apostles' teaching and fellowship, in the breaking of bread, and in the prayers;
- Persevere in resisting evil, and, when we fall into sin, repent and return to the Lord;
- Proclaim by word and example the Good News of God in Christ;
- Seek and serve Christ in all persons, loving our neighbors as ourselves;
- Strive for justice and peace among all people, respecting the dignity of every human being.

You'll notice that while the first two promises relate primarily to the interior work we do on ourselves, the other three require us to do ministry with others (well, the first one requires us to stay in fellowship, so that one needs a party too). This is our daily work. We all have to do this, every day.

We all live out these promises in different ways, depending on our character and our situation. C. S. Lewis calls for Christian economists to use Christian principles as they propose economic plans.[4] Teachers should remember these promises as they teach, parents as they parent, doctors as they doctor, engineers as they engineer. Being a baptized Christian is a full-time job. It covers everything. It's not something we do on Sundays or when we're feeling particularly self-righteous as we donate money to some especially worthy goal.

But some of us are called to take on additional duties. Not because we love God more or because God loves us more, but because, for a time, our best skills and talents match the needs of God's people in the church. And so, in addition to just existing, knowing that we are God's beloved and that our neighbors are too, loving God and loving our neighbor, some of us become acolytes. Some of us become lectors, some of us teach Sunday school, and some of us lead the church on the vestry.

Serving in Worship

Serving in worship is something anyone can do. Whether your congregation is big or small, high church or low, meets only on Sundays or has services every day of the week, there is a place for you to serve. Unlike most of the religions we see on TV, Christian worship is not performative. It is not something that the clergy can do on their own, without participation from a congregation. And the congregation's participation is not limited to "just listening attentively" either. We stand up, we sit down, we kneel, we chant, we respond. But if you are called to do a solo or small group role, there are lots of options. Let's start at the very front door.

Described herein are nearabout all the possible roles a worship service could include. Not every congregation will fill all these roles at every service. Some churches never have a subdeacon, for instance. But we're striving to be as comprehensive as possible here.

Greeter

Most churches have some kind person at the front door, sometimes handing out bulletins and prayer books, sometimes just saying hi and pointing the way to the restrooms. Church signage tends not to be super helpful, so having greeters really helps n00bs navigate their way around often ancient and labyrinthine buildings. You might be called to serve as a greeter if you're an extrovert, love meeting new people, and/or have empathy with folks who are new to this game.

Usher

Being an usher is awesome, because you get to hang out in the back the whole time. It's like being on the A/V team without actually having any buttons to push. Ushers pass out bulletins, help people find their seats, pass the plate for the offering, and guide people to the altar rail for communion. You might be called to serve as an usher if you like order, jobs that involve physical labor, and are the strong, silent type.

Acolyte

There are lots of subdivisions within acolytes, but let's start with a general overview. Acolytes serve the liturgical needs of the worship. They lead processions, light candles, help the priest set the table for communion, close the gate to the altar rail, assist in the ablutions, and generally help make everything more holy. Traditionally, acolytes tend to be children and teens, but there's no reason that has to be a hard and fast rule. You might be called to serve as an acolyte if you have good attention to detail, you like to keep moving during worship, or your piety runs to actions.

A <u>Verger</u> leads the procession, accompanied by a large, pointy stick. Historically, vergers were employed by large cathedrals to herd livestock out of the aisle. At least, that's the legend.

<u>Thurifers</u> provide the incense that demarcates worship as something holy, set apart for God. Different congregations use incense

in different ways and at different times, but a good thurifer keeps smoking hot coals in her thurible, a boat full of sweet-smelling incense, and a tight hand on the chains so that none of the fire goes flying.

Crucifer: A crucifer carries the cross. Following the cross is symbolic of our everyday life, so being a crucifer is one of the most important leadership roles. Often, the crucifer is also called upon to help in setting the altar for the Eucharist—pouring water and wine for the priest, washing his or her hands, and, in churches that do that sort of thing, ring the bells at the crucial moments.

Torch bearers always come in twos. They carry the light of Christ, the fire of the Holy Spirit, lighting the way of the procession. Like the vergers, they used to have a practical purpose: they lit the way through dark cathedral passages, they illuminated the pages of the Gospel as it was read. Now, they represent the light of Christ that has come into our world.

Lector

Lectors read the Word of God to the people, which is essential. The lector reads the lessons, from the Old Testament and the New. You need a strong, confident voice that can declaim the words of the Scripture with authority and passion, without straying into over-dramatization. The poetry and rhythm of the words will support you—assuming you aren't trying to cold-read them. Must be comfortable in front of a crowd.

Musician

Music is not required at every service of worship, but nearly all churches incorporate it in at least their primary services. Augustine of Hippo (354–430 CE) said that he who sings prays twice, and the power of music to move a congregation to awe, reverence, penitence, elation, and glory cannot be overstated. Different churches (and sometimes different services at the same church) will have different musicians serving in various roles.

One typically sees, in Episcopal churches, a choir accompanied by organ, but of course many churches use piano or guitar as their primary accompaniment, and you could even see a praise team. The type of music is less important than the way the music serves the community: inspiring courage, inviting the congregation into the otherworldly presence of God, knitting together the souls of those present into the One Body of Christ that they are. To this end, congregational and choral music (that is to say, music that is done together) are preferable to solo music of any genre.

But solos and instrumental music do have their place; in seminary, this author worshipped at an entirely non-participatory service that was sung entirely by four voices, alone and in concert. The church was dark, lit only by candles illuminating the altar, so we could not see the singers, and we were invited to join in their song only by listening, by letting our hearts be strangely warmed by what they conveyed. In many churches, you see this done during communion so that the people's hearts might be drawn to the Feast of the Lord as they journey forward to break bread together on their knees. The talents necessary to serve as a musician are well known, I think, so I will not list them. Needless to say, if you are an organist, offering your services at a contemporary service would be less well received; vice versa, if you are a rock guitarist.

Eucharistic Minister

These servants at the altar of God have one of the most essential roles of all: bearing the cup of Christ to the faithful at communion. They wait, patiently, throughout the Liturgy of the Word, pray silently with the priest as she presides at the Eucharistic Prayer, then step forward to convey the holy chalice, filled with the blood of Christ, to the people. Eucharistic Minister is a public role, a role at the front of the church, but it is also a largely silent role, breaking that silence only for the murmured assurance, "The Blood of Christ, the cup of salvation" to the one receiving that cup. It is full of responsibility: the chalice bearer must protect the cup from spilling, assist the drinker, consume or properly dispose of any remaining wine. Despite its silence, it is a central role, necessary for any Eucharist to take place.

Subdeacon

The subdeacon also serves at the altar of God, with even greater power and even greater responsibility. As subdeacon (which translates from a weird Latin-Greek hybrid to "under-servant" in English), you assist the priest and the deacon, if there is one, by reading the second lesson, by bearing the Gospel book for the gospeller, by pointing the altar book during the Eucharist, and bearing a chalice at communion. Unlike the Eucharistic Ministers, who can veg out for the vast majority of the service, there is always something for the subdeacon to do: reading, carrying, receiving offerings, pointing, and serving. Some churches omit this role and divide its tasks among other leaders. A second lector could read the second lesson, of course, and many priests follow the altar book on their own without someone to point for them, particularly if that priest doesn't observe too many manual acts and bows that would take their eyes away from the book. But in churches that have subdeacons, the role is best suited to someone who cares very deeply about ensuring that the Eucharist goes smoothly and someone who enjoys being at the center of the action in a servant, assisting role. Maybe someone who enjoys wearing pretty vestments too.

Eucharistic Visitor

Eucharistic Visitors do some of the most important and most scripturally-based work in the service. The Acts of the Apostles tells us that, "Now during those days, when the disciples were increasing in number, the Hellenists complained against the Hebrews because their widows were being neglected in the daily distribution of food."[5] In nearly every community, there will be some who are unable to be present at the table for reasons they did not choose, such as the elderly, those recovering from surgery, and new mothers. It is essential that the church provide for their participation in the Great Supper of the Lamb, the Holy Eucharist, by sending forth visitors from the table, to take to them our greetings in the name of the Lord, the good Word proclaimed to us that day, and the Blessed Sacrament, to be received at home. In being sent forth from that very Table in which we all share in the body and blood of Christ, the visitors make really present the community of the faithful with whom these homebound share the Feast. Visiting the sick and infirm requires a cheerful, open heart willing to make the sacrifice of time to include these beloved in God in our worship.

Serving the Church Beyond Worship

The rituals of the Church are profoundly important. They make Christ really present with us, and they offer the congregation direct communion with God. But the Church exists beyond worship, and needs the laity to serve, lead, teach, and give seven whole days, not one in seven.[6]

Teacher

Too often, the teacher conjures the image of our least favorite public school teacher: stern, uncompromising, writing a lesson on the board. Or the stereotype of a strict old nun in full habit, ready with her ruler to whack you if you don't remember your verse. Nothing could be further from the truth. Think of a teacher like Mr. Miyagi: They hold the secrets to the wisdom of the universe through a lifetime of discipline and practice. If you pay attention, you just might learn something.

Stephen Minister[7]

Not every church has Stephen Ministers, but nearly every one has some kind of pastoral caregiver—someone to walk beside those in the parish who are in need, suffering, or in any kind of trouble.[8] Stephen Ministers aren't therapists. They're not social workers. They're not fixers. They're not going to make the problem better. Their job is to share the burden, like two oxen bearing the weight of the same yoke. Stephen Ministers should be kind, compassionate, caregiving individuals who are generous with their time (and circumspect with the confidential information they learn). Definitely not for rogues.

Vestry

These are the council elders. The leaders of the community, charged with the responsibility to make good decisions for the mission of the church. Vestry members have fiduciary (that's financial, nerds) responsibility for church-owned buildings and financial holdings. Vestry is an elected position, and term-limited.

Within the vestry, there are two wardens with especial responsibilities. They get called different names at different churches, but usually the senior warden is chosen by the rector, and works closely with her in leading the vestry, making administrative decisions, choosing search committees for the new rector, and so on. The senior warden is in charge when the rector's away. The junior warden has responsibility over the physical plant—all the buildings, the grounds, property stuff. That's who you call when the building floods or you find a nest of copperheads in the elevator shaft (this actually happened to a friend of mine—she needed help to get those mother effin' snakes out of the mother effin' elevator).[9]

Delegate to Diocesan Convention

Every year, the diocese meets in convention. We'll talk more about General Convention in a later chapter [see "Comic-Con Lite" on page 106]: Diocesan convention is like a mini version of the General Convention. Depending on its size, each church elects a number of laypeople to represent it to the rest of the diocese. These delegates vote on diocesan-wide policy, elect leadership of the diocese (including a new bishop, when needed), and stand for election to leadership themselves. This is a job for the wonks. The political nerds. The rules lawyers who can read through the impenetrable legalese behind each resolution, and who are willing to stand up and fight for their interpretation to prevail. Gamers, this one's for you.

[Skip to "Comic-Con Lite," page 106, to learn more about General Convention.]

The Clergy

One mistake many observers—and even Christians—make is to assume that clergy are somehow better, holier, or closer to God than the laity. Nothing could be further from the truth. Clergy are the ordained ministers of the Church. They have been called out by God to be re-ordered, to be placed in a particular type of ministry. They are entrusted with great power, and hold great responsibility. Therefore, we rightly spend a great deal of time discerning whom God is calling to serve in this way, whereas baptism is open to absolutely anybody. There are three orders of clerical ministry: the diaconate, the priesthood (sometimes called the presbyterate), and the episcopate (that's bishops).

Deacons

The word "deacon" comes from the Greek word for servant. At heart, deacon ministry is a servant ministry. The first deacons were appointed by the twelve apostles to make sure that the widows and orphans who were Greeks and not Jews got their share at the Holy Potlucks that were the very first Eucharists held by the church in Acts. Their first job, ever, was to serve, and to serve specifically the people who were most likely to be forgotten or ignored by the rest of the church.

Deacon ministry, then, is servant ministry, and it's also a ministry of reminders. A deacon's job is to keep reminding the rest of us to look out for those whom we would rather forget. It's a thankless job, really, this constant Cassandra-ing, this nagging everyone to be better. They say that activism is what moves the needle in justice movements, but that nobody really likes activists. They're not often pleasant to be around. Deacons are (or should be) like that.

In the service where a deacon is ordained, the bishop offers the following examination:

My *brother*, every Christian is called to follow Jesus Christ, serving God the Father, through the power of the Holy Spirit. God now calls you to a special ministry of servanthood directly under your bishop. In the name of Jesus Christ, you are to serve all people, particularly the poor, the weak, the sick, and the lonely.

As a deacon in the Church, you are to study the Holy Scriptures, to seek nourishment from them, and to model your life upon them. You are to make Christ and his redemptive love known, by your word and example, to those among whom you live, and work, and worship. You are to interpret to the Church the needs, concerns, and hopes of the world. You are to assist the bishop and priests in public worship and in the ministration of God's Word and Sacraments, and you are to carry out other duties assigned to you from time to time. At all times, your life and teaching are to show Christ's people that in serving the helpless they are serving Christ himself.[10]

In the Book of Common Prayer, anytime a pronoun or title like *brother* is used, the use of italics indicates that the applicable gender should be used. Sadly, these pronouns are nearly always masculine, displaying a prejudice towards male subjects as the norm. There is only one prayer in which feminine pronouns are used as normative, the third Collect of a Martyr on page 247 (page 195 for traditional language).

The diaconate is a lifelong, special ministry that requires being set apart. That's what the word "holy" means, originally, set apart. To be ordained deacon is to join the clergy, which means a life of obedience and sacrifice. Being a deacon is particularly sacrificial, because it is typically a non-stipendiary (that is, unpaid) position. The examination asks the deacon to enter this special ministry and calls out its specific tasks:

- Deacons serve directly under the bishop. They don't owe priests any obedience or loyalty (as much as priests might wish that were so). Their ministry is not centered in a congregation, but could take them anywhere.

- Deacons serve a particular group of people: the poor, the weak, the sick, and the lonely. In this, they prove that they are the most like God of all the orders. Liberation theologians claim that God has a "preferential option for the poor," and the Roman Catholic Church has accepted that as true doctrine. This means that while God loves everyone, and saves everyone, there is a particular soft spot in God's heart for those who experience material poverty, as Scripture attests. Deacons serve the poor, those whom God loves best, so they are the closest to and most like God of all of us.

- Like the rest of the clergy, deacons are to take the time to really immerse themselves in the Scriptures.

- Here is the crux of the deacon's call: "You are to interpret to the Church the needs, hopes, and concerns of the world."[11] Deacons must serve out in the world, and remind the Church, too often in our little Christian bubble, what the world is asking for. A diaconal ministry is almost like an undercover operation; the deacon lives in the world among them, serving them, and then returns to base to tell the Church what the community needs. To be a deacon is to be a prophet, crying out in the wilderness, naming the places where the Church has fallen short of God's commandments. It is precisely because the diaconal ministry is a servant ministry that deacons are able to do this—how can a bishop, one of the ruling princes of the Church, declare its faults and need for change? He is the one in charge, the one with privilege, the one unable to see past his churchly bubble. How can a priest, caught up in the duties of running a parish, away from those who haven't set foot in a church in years, tell the Church how to mend our ways? We need deacons, those who are not rulers, those who are in some sense outside us, to set us aright.

- At all times, deacons remind us of Jesus's story about the End of Days in Matthew 25. Jesus gathers the nations before him and welcomes those who have fed him when he was hungry, welcomed him when he was a stranger, and visited him when he was sick and in prison. These folks are perplexed. They don't believe they have ever seen Jesus in such a weak position. Jesus responds that whatever they have done for the "least of these," they did for him. Mother Theresa didn't serve lepers because she believed Jesus commanded her to; she served lepers because she believed that, in some sense, they were Jesus. St. Martin of Tours gave half his cloak to a freezing beggar, then had a vision in which the beggar was Christ. Deacons remind us of this, when we would rather forget.

All priests must serve as deacons for a minimum of six months before they can be ordained as priests in the Episcopal Church. There are some who believe this is silly; if one knows one is called to be a priest, why pretend and serve in a different order for this short time? Others think it is worse—that it devalues the work of a deacon by implying a hierarchy, as though the diaconate is a step on a journey to leadership and those who are called to remain deacons forever are somehow less than, as though the priest has mastered what it means to be a deacon in a mere six months.

I disagree. Spending a period of time (I wish it were longer) in servant ministry, working directly with the poor, the weak, the sick, and the lonely, is essential to forming future priests who will stand *in persona Christi* at the altar of God. Once someone is ordained a priest, she does not lose her status as a deacon. She carries with her into her priestly ministry that charism, that duty to call attention to those who would otherwise be forgotten. Just because that is no longer her primary or most visible ministry does not mean it is not a crucial part of her identity.

A **charism** is a special grace, unique to a person or a group of people.

Furthermore, it is absolutely vital for our bishops to carry within themselves all four orders of ministry. They are the ultimate hybrid class, the only ones who have served as laypeople, bishops, priests, and deacons, and thus can relate to every single Christian they encounter. When they take their stand as the rulers in the Church, they must be grounded with the knowledge that within themselves they carry all of us. To bypass diaconal ordination for priests would leave deacons out of this embodiment, which would impoverish us all.

Priests

Priests are the most visible of the "professional classes" of Christians. They're the ones up at the front in church on Sunday, making the sign of the cross at the door. Priests are the ones presiding at the altar, baptizing babies, officiating marriages and funerals. They tend to wear a clerical collar (more often than their diaconal brethren and sistren, most of whom have secular jobs when they're not at church), and so when you are thinking of "clergy," the person in your imagination is probably a priest.

 [You can skip to see their cosplay in "Vestments," page 72, but come back.]

But what is a priest? What is their job? What does it look like to see a priest in action? The priest has many responsibilities, all of which are rooted, like the deacon's, in the examination we give them are their ordination.

> My *brother*, the Church is the family of God, the body of Christ, and the temple of the Holy Spirit. All baptized people are called to make Christ known as Savior and Lord, and to share in the renewing of his world. Now you are called to work as pastor, priest, and teacher, together with your bishop and fellow presbyters, and to take your share in the councils of the Church.
>
> As a priest, it will be your task to proclaim by word and deed the Gospel of Jesus Christ, and to fashion your life in

accordance with its precepts. You are to love and serve the people among whom you work, caring alike for young and old, strong and weak, rich and poor. You are to preach, to declare God's forgiveness to penitent sinners, to pronounce God's blessing, to share in the administration of Holy Baptism and in the celebration of the mysteries of Christ's Body and Blood, and to perform the other ministrations entrusted to you. In all that you do, you are to nourish Christ's people from the riches of his grace, and to strengthen them to glorify God in this life and in the life to come."[12]

The story of **Melchizedek** is a strange one, from the book of Genesis. After rescuing his nephew Lot, who had been captured by Chedorlaomer, king of Elam, Abraham is blessed by a strange king—Melchizedek of Salem. Scripture tells us that Melchizedek was a priest of "God Most High," a formulation that usually refers exclusively to the Jewish God, whom we Christians call God the Father. But Melchizedek was not a Jew. He is not a descendent of Abraham (obvs), and he does not live according to the Law of Moses (since it hasn't been written yet). But he blesses Abraham, and Abraham responds by giving him one-tenth of everything that he owns—the first tithe. In both Jewish and Christian tradition, Melchizedek represents an order of priests outside the tribe of Levi, the descendants of Moses's brother Aaron. A priest in the order of Melchizedek is a priest outside the genetic line. Jesus, being from the family of David (and the tribe of Judah), is a priest in the order of Melchizedek, and so too are all these Gentiles who follow him as Christian priests.

Priesthood is also a lifelong order. The Scripture verse we use comes from Hebrews, "You are a priest forever, according to the order of Melchizedek."[13] Unless a priest commits a heinous crime, worthy of being inhibited[14] or defrocked, nothing can take her priesthood away. To be a priest is to live a life devoted to God, and to making God known to God's people. A priest works as a *pastor*, that is to say a shepherd of God's people. Pastors have a responsibility to encourage, support, challenge, and lead the people in the way of the Lord. God holds them responsible for the welfare of the people, morally and substantively.[15] A priest works as a *priest*, presiding at the altar of God, offering sacrifices of praise and thanksgiving to God the Father. Priests officiate sacraments. Priests facilitate the relationship between humanity and the Divine. It is a holy—and supernatural—calling, one fraught with challenge and weighted with magic.

The **reputation of the priesthood** has been tarnished in recent years by revelations of horrific sexual abuse, most famously in the Roman Catholic Church, but there is not a denomination in Christendom that does not have its share of abusers. The Episcopal Church is not exempt. Priestly responsibilities often require confidentiality, one-on one-meetings, and when enabled by a culture that supports the authority of the priest, assumes their innocence and trusts their word, it is possible for abuse to flourish. This is a great sin, for which the Church continues to repent (some days more effectively than others).

Finally, a priest works as a *teacher*, encouraging and guiding the people in her charge as they seek to understand God more truly.

A priest also:

- Takes her share in the councils of the church. While the Episcopal Church is hierarchical (a priest also swears to obey her bishop and all other ministers who may have authority over her and her work), part of a priest's job is to contribute her voice to church leadership. Obedience is not unthinking compliance; rather, a priest's obedience to Christ requires her to advocate strongly for those whom we sinful humans would otherwise forget. Priests are, by necessity, in the room where it happens, and must bring with them the voices of those who are not.

- The next line sounds a little ridiculous—the Baptismal Covenant requires all of us to proclaim by word and example the Good News of Jesus Christ, and to fashion our lives in accordance with the precepts of the Gospel. But priests are asked to pay special attention to this, for two reasons. First, because they're so visible. As the most public face of the church, and as the ones asked to stand in the place of Christ at the communion table, priests represent God to many people. They have a responsibility to publicly hold themselves accountable. (Including when they screw up. Priests are still human, after all.) Secondly, because the Church invests them with a great deal of authority. And with that authority comes the potential for abuse. With great power comes great responsibility, after all.

- Unlike deacons, priests don't have a special mandate regarding for whom they should care. Deacons are supposed to care for the poor. Priests are supposed to care equally for everyone. No discrimination—everyone counts.

- Preaching isn't limited to priests; there are licensed lay preachers (and darn good ones), but all priests are called to preach. If priests are to mediate the Divine presence to the people, part of that duty involves interpreting the Word of God as contained in the Old and New Testaments.

- Priests are granted the authority to declare God's forgiveness to penitent sinners in a sacramental way, above and beyond the assurances that deacons and laypersons can offer. While many find that unburdening themselves by confessing their sins to any other person can be helpful, the Church teaches that only priests are sacramentally able to declare unequivocal absolution. This absolution can be offered to a general confession, like we do in church on Sunday, or in private, auricular confession, the kind you see on TV in the little curtained booths.

- Priests declare God's blessing. God's blessing is always present; priests acknowledge what is already true and therefore make manifest the blessing of God. It is not a sacrament, but it is a holy thing, and while it is not dependent on the personal holiness of the priest (thank goodness), it requires the set-apart-ness of priesthood.

- Priests and bishops are the only ones who, except in case of emergency, can administer baptism and Holy Eucharist. And it is their duty to do so; different churches have different practices regarding how often both are made available to the people, but it needs to be more than never.

I've never heard of an emergency Eucharist, but I suppose if there were vampires coming after you or something. . . .

- In all that they do, priests must partake of the nourishment of Christ's grace, and offer that grace to others. One cannot give away what one does not have. In order for a priest to facilitate the interactions between God and humankind, she must build and maintain her own connection with God. She must be fervent in prayer and faithful in study. She must regularly partake of the sacraments herself, not just administer them for others. But neither may she hoard God's grace for herself, and demand from the people what she does not hold to herself. It's a tricky tightrope to walk, and she can only manage it through that grace. Ergo, the praying.

Parish or congregation—all are a church community, one unit of Christians who gather on the Lord's Day for worship and fellowship.

Priesthood is the class, but within it there are many roles. Being a priest is a lifelong gig. What kind of priest you might be changes over many years of ministry. The foundation of priestly ministry is the congregation (sometimes called a parish). At your church, your priest could be called by any of the following titles:

Rector

This is the senior priest of a church that can afford to pay her. Rectors have tenure; they can only be let go in cases of misconduct or extreme disharmony with their community. It is their duty to lead the community, to challenge it to more fully live the Gospel, and to grow its reach, both into the hearts of its members or beyond its doors.

Priest-in-Charge

Sometimes called a **vicar**, this is the bishop's representative, *vicarius* meaning "substitute" from Latin, and acts in his place in a missionary community. Most often the bishop appoints them, as the church can't afford to pay a salary. The vicar as second-in-command may be the title of a senior associate priest at a large parish, too. Priests-in-charge don't have tenure, and they answer to the bishop, not to their community, but in all other ways they have the same mission as rectors.

The **Church** doesn't build communities exclusively based on who can afford a full-time priest.

Curate

A new priest, serving as a sort of "trainee associate." Like a medical resident. They're fully priests and can perform all the sacraments just as much as their senior colleagues, but they are under the guidance of a senior priest who helps to form them early in their ministry.

Ordained Orders of Another Dimension

The local congregation is the foundation of all church life, but there are certainly roles for priests outside the parish. Such as:

Chaplain

A chaplain is the minister of a chapel, instead of a church. You can find chapels in all kinds of places; historically rich people and nobility had them in their houses. Today, chapels are more commonly found in hospitals and schools. Hospital chaplaincy and school chaplaincy are quite different in the skills they require, but both jobs go by the same name. Go figure.

Chapel comes from the Old French for *cape*, and means "sanctuary for relics." St. Martin of Tours (in France) was well known for having shared his cloak with a beggar who ended up being Jesus. The part of the cloak he retained was later cut up and shared in "chapels" all over France so that Christians everywhere could be close to the great saint.

Canon

Canons serve as ministers of the diocese, either on the diocese-wide staff or at a cathedral. Lay canons exist, but it's atypical. Canons are associates to either the bishop or to the:

Dean

Dean has a three-fold meaning, besting chaplain by at least one meaning. A dean could be: (1) the head of an academic institution, such as a seminary or theological college; (2) the senior priest of a cathedral, serving as "rector" at the bishop's seat and offering ministry to the whole diocese; or (3) an elected or appointed middle manager over a region within a diocese.

Non-Parochial

Priests who work outside a parish or a cathedral are called "non-parochial" (that's just Latin for not-parish). This applies to chaplains (above), and also to priests who serve in untraditional capacities—as executive director for a non-profit, for example, or a professor at a university or teacher in a school. They're still a priest, still under the authority of their bishop, and must report to her about how they are living into their call to serve God as a priest.

Priests Serve in Worship, Too

Just like laypersons, there are lots of different roles for priests (assuming more than one is present) during worship. Any priest can serve in any role—once you're ordained priest, there's no leveling up, at least not in worship. These roles include:

Presider/Celebrant

This priest is the one who presides over the Eucharistic Prayer. They get to wear the *chasuble* (see page 76). They are the one who goes last in procession (which means that really they're most important, since Jesus said the last shall be first). They pray the Eucharistic Prayer and consecrate the bread and the wine. They are sometimes called the celebrant, because they celebrate the Eucharist, the Mass. But in more recent days, liturgical scholars have argued that we all celebrate the Eucharist together, so a more appropriate word is presider. They act *in persona Christi*, in the person of Christ, as the host of this Holy Meal.

Preacher

Can be a licensed layperson or deacon, but is usually a priest. This person gives the sermon. They may or may not play a role in the eucharistic portion of worship.

Gospeller

If no deacon is present to read the Gospel, then a priest will do so. Deacons are particularly called to read the Gospel in worship, as the prophetic proclaimers of Christ's Good News to all hearers. Since priests contain within themselves the diaconate as well, it is possible for them to read the Gospel in the absence of a deacon.

Assisting Priest

The deck-swabbers. These priests have no official duties, but work very hard behind the scenes to wrangle acolytes, cue Eucharistic Ministers, and fetch and carry anything that might have been forgotten but is necessary for the service.

Bishops

The successors of the apostles. The princes of the church. The HBICs. The guys with the big pointy hats. The word "bishop" comes from an Old English bastardization of the Greek word *episkopos*—the same word that forms "episcopal." So the Episcopal Church is one that places a pretty high value on bishops.

In the Episcopal Church and some other provinces of the Anglican Communion, the people of the diocese elect their bishops. Priests, who can come from absolutely anywhere in the church—including from other Anglican provinces—are selected by a nominating committee to let their name stand for election. The candidates for election go on "walkabout," the fancy name for a series of meetings held around the diocese with laypersons, deacons, and priests. They ask questions of the candidates, discerning their fit for the diocese. Then, guided by the Holy Spirit, they hold an election. An honest-to-God election with secret ballots and everything. The candidate who is elected prepares for ordination to the episcopate.[16] The candidates who aren't go back to being priests.

At their ordination[17] and consecration,[18] bishops are given the following examination:

> My *brother*, the people have chosen you and have affirmed their trust in you by acclaiming your election. A bishop in God's holy Church is called to be one with the apostles in proclaiming Christ's resurrection and interpreting the Gospel, and to testify to Christ's sovereignty as Lord of lords and King of kings.
>
> You are called to guard the faith, unity, and discipline of the Church; to celebrate and to provide for the administration of the sacraments of the New Covenant; to ordain priests and deacons and to join in ordaining bishops; and to be in all things a faithful pastor and wholesome example for the entire flock of Christ.
>
> With your fellow bishops you will share in the leadership of the Church throughout the world. Your heritage is the faith of patriarchs, prophets, apostles, and martyrs, and those of every generation who have looked to God in hope. Your joy will be to follow him who came, not to be served, but to serve, and to give his life a ransom for many.[19]

Episcopal: When it's the lower-case "e," it means "bishop-ly;" upper-case "E" means part of the Episcopal Church.

The episcopate, like the priesthood and the diaconate, is a life-long order. Some bishops decide to retire from leading a diocese, and these can accept positions teaching at or administrating seminaries, or even serving in parishes again. They remain bishops, though, no matter their work. There are some complicated rules about episcopal authority, and how bishops can exercise their ministry when outside the diocese they are bishop of—and these apply to these retired bishops too.

But let's take a look at that examination:

- Priests and deacons discern their call in consultation with mentors, rectors, commissions, and bishops. The people consent to their ordination at that ordination. Bishop discernment, however, involves an election. They are chosen directly by the people, who affirm their trust in that bishop's leadership.

- Bishops, even more than the rest of us, are the successors of Jesus's twelve apostles. They have apostolic authority to ordain additional ministers of the gospel, to decide where the mission of God should go next. Bishops must interpret the Gospel for the world around them, and testify that while they have apostolic authority, it proceeds from the One who has all the authority, all the sovereignty: Jesus Christ.

- A bishop's primary duty is to guard the faith, unity, and discipline of the Church. This is a heavy burden to bear. Bishops serve as shepherds of the people, and we all know that guiding people can be herding cats at times. There are many who are not faithful. There are many who do not care about unity. There are many who resent or reject discipline. But a bishop is called to continue on.

- Bishops ensure that the sacraments of the New Covenant (baptism and the Eucharist) will be administered in their jurisdiction.

- Bishops are called upon to ordain priests and deacons, and to ensure that there are adequate laborers for ministering to the harvest of God. They are also required to assist in ordaining bishops—it takes three bishops to make a bishop, in our tradition. No rogue bishop can run off and ordain more bishops without the help of his sisters and brothers. Properly, the presiding bishop should serve as one of these ordaining bishops, but he can appoint a representative to take his place when needed.

- A bishop must be a faithful pastor and wholesome example for all in her charge. Like priests, the intent here is not to put her on a pedestal or assume that she is somehow more than human, but rather to recognize that if she is to preach the Gospel, there must be some evidence for that Gospel in her life.

- Bishops share with other bishops in the leadership of the Church in the world. Here's a secret: Bishop is top of the line, at least in The Episcopal Church. Presiding bishops and archbishops may preside at the table, but bishops are not bound in obedience to them the way that priests are duty-bound to obey their bishop in all that is not sin.

I say bishops are top of the line; one might say instead that they are at the bottom. The Church is a downwardly mobile institution. As you ascend to greater leadership, you accept a heavier cross to bear. As we tell bishops, "Your joy will be to follow him who came not to be served but to serve, and to give his life a ransom for many."[20] Bishops, even more than anyone else, by virtue of the great power they wield, must follow the example of Jesus Christ,

> who, though he was in the form of God,
> > did not regard equality with God
> > as something to be exploited,
> but emptied himself,
> > taking the form of a slave,
> > being born in human likeness.

And being found in human form,
   he humbled himself
   and became obedient to the point of death—
   even death on a cross.[21]

So those are the four classes. Which do you feel called to play?

Vestments
The Cosplay Section of Church

In which quite a number of pretty vestments are worn

 [If cosplay isn't your bag, skip to the next chapter on page 79 to equip your character.]

Now, most folks I've gamed with don't cosplay at the table—that's what minis are for. We're not LARPers,[1] for goodness' sake. But even those of us who turn our noses up at our good friends the LARPers might indulge in some cosplay at Comic-Con or for a superhero party or something.

The Church has many opportunities for cosplay. A church might dispense with *vestments* (that's a general term for any kind of special robe, hat, or accessory) in the heat of the summer, but typically, anyone who has a role "upfront" will be wearing something special. Some of these vestments demark one's *order*, which is fairly permanent. Others show one's role in the service, which nearly always varies from week to week. As a priest, I get to wear a special outfit at nearly every single service. Here are a few options you might see on a regular basis.

Cassock

The cassock is basic wear for most people, clergy and lay, participating in the service. Choir members, chalice bearers, and clergy all might wear one. It may be worn at both eucharistic and non-eucharistic services. It is a plain, black robe with a high neck and long sleeves that finishes at your ankle. Think Professor McGonagall (I've totally worn my cassock to dress up as her on Halloween). It goes under most other vestments. It gives you +2 against "Fear of Death." When worn under an alb, adds +2 to "Things we do because they're tradition, not because they make any sense."

Surplice

A surplice is a short white robe worn over (and only over) a cassock. It cannot be worn alone. It is worn at both eucharistic and non-eucharistic services, but never by the *celebrant* at the Eucharist. [Go to "Presider/Celebrant" on page 67 of the "Classes" chapter.] There are lots of different styles of surplice, namely the:

- "Old English": Long, droopy sleeves give you cathedral-grade gravitas as you swish your way through the procession. +1 to Charisma.
- "American": These short-sleeved, practical surplices give you automatic Freedom of Movement. Highly recommended for *thurifers*.
- "Cotta": What makes a cotta? The lace. Lots and lots of lace. Add extra lace for only 10 GP per panel, with the bonus of infuriating cardinals who fear the feminization of the church.

Hood

An academic drapery that gives no shelter from weather. -2 to Survival, unless you have Endure Elements (also known as: a cloak). This indicates the education of the wearer (usually clergy and musicians) to at least the Masters level. Requires +2 Intelligence.

Tippet

Tippets are easily confused with *stoles* (see below), given that they're both long strips of cloth worn round the neck and hang

down the front. A tippet, though, is black. Stoles are rarely, if ever, black. Tippets are *only* worn at non-eucharistic services, by any ordained clergy, or anyone serving in a preaching or officiant role. Wearers may choose to add seals of their seminary alma mater and/or the diocese in which they serve. (NB: In England, this gives you a -1 to Charisma. Apparently it's not The Thing.)

Preaching Tabs

Those goofy little white strips that hang down from the collar in all the paintings of old-timey preachers. These are what we call *adiaphora*—unimportant. Wear them, or don't, as you choose. They give no bonuses and receive no penalties. Whatever floats your boat, preacher man (or woman).

Cappa Nigra

The Latin word for a giant, heavy black cloak to be worn for outdoor services (specifically graveside) when it's freezing out. Unlike most vestments, this garment primarily serves a practical, rather than ceremonial, use. Grants unlimited Endure Elements.

Alb

Hoo boy. Time to wade into a little bit of Episcopal controversy. Here goes: An alb is historically a thin, white cotton or linen garment, worn over the cassock by the celebrant of the Eucharist. In the twentieth century, an enterprising vestment-maker invented the cassock-alb, a thicker white cotton/polyester blend that can be worn without a cassock under it (it's not see-through). There is a large portion of the Episcopal Church that regards the cassock-alb with a horror usually reserved for those who think that Luke Skywalker and the *Enterprise* inhabit the same universe. It is anathema to them. When in a game run by a DM with such feelings, make sure to express your hatred for this garment as often as possible for extra XP.

Those of us more pragmatically inclined just wear a cassock-alb. +2 to Will saves against Fear of Change.

This garment can also be worn by *acolytes*.

Scapular

This long, flat piece of cloth is usually associated with *religious*, which is the jargon-y term for monks and nuns. However, at my church, acolytes also wear them. They come in various colors to match the liturgical season, and are worn over a cassock-alb. These are great for hiding your hands under when you don't want someone to see that you're signaling to steal third base.

Yes, the Episcopal Church has **monks** and **nuns**, too. Vowed religious orders are not just for Roman Catholics. Religious can be any order: lay, deacon, priest, or bishop, and they can vest or not vest, depending on their Rule of Life.

Stole

The yoke of Christ, which is an easy burden and light.[2] Worn by clergy who have made lifelong ordination vows to carry out a particular sacramental ministry, when exercising that ministry. Stoles are usually only worn at services that include a sacrament (baptism, Eucharist, a funeral, a wedding), and are worn by every ordained person exercising their ministry in that service, not just the presider (see "Presider/Celebrant" on page 67).

- Deacons: A deacon stole is worn diagonally across the chest, in the opposite direction to a sash worn in beauty pageants. This stole symbolizes the proclamation of the Word of God and the servant ministry to which deacons are particularly called.
- Priests: A priest's stole is worn around the neck, like a yoke, symbolizing that priests have taken on the yoke of Christ.

Chasuble

A large poncho-like garment worn over a cassock-alb (or cassock + alb) and stole. Worn only by the celebrant at the Eucharist. Does not confer any powers on its own, but demonstrates that the wearer has the authority to preside at the Eucharist. Changes color to match the liturgical season.

Dalmatic

This long, one-piece garment with sleeves and two embroidered bars (one across the chest, the other across the knees) is worn at the Eucharist by deacons, or priests exercising their diaconal role in a Eucharistic service. It is worn over cassock-alb (or cassock + alb) and stole. Changes color to match the liturgical season.

Tunical

The same as a dalmatic, but with only one embroidered bar across the chest. It is worn at the Eucharist by subdeacons. It should match the color of the chasuble and dalmatic, as these three sacred ministers are all presiding together at the altar.

Cope

A giant fancy-looking cape that every priest longs to wear just as much as some little girls dream about their wedding dresses. Worn on special occasions by the celebrant, and most frequently by bishops. Picture the "mawwwwidge" guy from *The Princess Bride*. He's wearing a cope.

Mitre

The mawwwidge guy? He's also wearing a mitre, which is a tall, pointy hat that is only worn by bishops, and only at specific points in the service. Giving a blessing? Wear the mitre. Saying a prayer? Don't wear the mitre. The mitre etiquette is tricky and fraught with controversy. A few years ago, Presiding Bishop Katharine Jefferts Schori was invited to preach at Southwark Cathedral in London. She was asked not to wear her mitre in worship. The official reason given was that she was out of her jurisdiction, but many suspected the real reason was that women could not be ordained bishop at that time in England. The story goes that she carried it in her hand the whole service. Bishops—mess with their mitres at your peril.

Canterbury Cap

This snazzy-looking cap, like the *cappa nigra*, originally had a practical purpose. It was cold in sixteenth century cathedrals in England

(it often still is). The Canterbury cap is divided into four parts, and was specifically developed to look different from the Roman Catholic biretta, so don't be fooled. The Canterbury cap is the Episcopal way. This cap is suitable for all clergy, and there are a number of different colors available. Basic black is the way to go, though.

Crozier

In addition to copes and mitres, bishops also get to carry big sticks. As a symbol of their position as shepherd of their diocese, they carry a big shepherd's crook. In olden days, these were often covered in multi-colored jewels, and in the basement of Canterbury cathedral, you can see the exquisite materials. But these days, most bishops choose wisely and go with a simple wooden stick.

Equipment
Fire and Big Sticks

In which the reader is equipped with the tools for ministry

 [After you've equipped your character, go back to page 72 to choose the proper "Vestments" for each role.]

Over two thousand years, hundreds of cultures have given the Church a ton of equipment options to use in our rituals. Obviously, churches differ in how many of these they use. Churches that identify as "high church" or "Anglo-Catholic" will typically use more pieces of equipment than those who identify as "low church" or "evangelical." Using fewer pieces of equipment is not a sign of a n00b; it is a theological and liturgical choice deserving of respect. That said, as a geek, I highly encourage you to use as many pieces of equipment as possible, mostly because they're really stinking cool.

Anglo-Catholicism grew up in Oxford, England, in the early nineteenth century. The Tractarians, so-called because they wrote many tracts (original), admired Roman Catholic practices and wished that the Church of England might return to such things as the use of candles on the altar and private, sacramental confession. Churches and individuals across the Anglican Communion may self-identify as Anglo-Catholic.

Thurible

A top-notch smoke bomb that physicalizes the prayers of the church that they may rise before God as incense. It is swung on a long chain in a number of patterns, depending on the skill of the thurifer. Does a d8+5 Holy damage—not Fire. Its incense is cleansing and purifying, rather than destructive. The thurifer leads processions, censes the Gospel, the altar, the gifts of bread and wine, the presider, and the people. This marks each of those—the space, the Gospel, the altar, the eucharistic elements, the presider, and the people—as holy and acceptable to God, set apart from the everyday world.

Boat

A boat holds the incense and is carried throughout the service to refresh the thurible, not unlike a quiver full of arrows. Sometimes, there is a boat boy (or girl), usually the youngest and smallest and cutest of the acolytes, who carries the boat for the thurifer, but the thurifer can usually manage in the absence of an adorable moppet.

In the Episcopal Church, liturgical style is designated by confusing terms such as high, low, or broad church. A high church is not one that's got a tall steeple or is on top of a mountain. Rather, it is a church that values the aesthetic appeal of worship in the beauty of holiness. This worship will be somewhat more complicated. The presider may face the altar, away from the people (this is called "east-facing," since most churches are built such that the altar faces eastward). There will probably be incense, at least on high feast days. The vestments will be fancier, a little more precious. A low church values the simplicity of worshipping without so much visual stimulation. There is less iconography. The vestments are simpler. Chanting is unlikely. Broad church grew up in the mid- to late-twentieth century as a way to designate churches that felt they were in the middle of these two groups. As such, it is such a broad term (pun intended) that discovering its actual meaning is difficult.

Torch

Pretty self-explanatory. A torch is a large, portable candle, carried by acolytes flanking each cross in the procession. They always come in pairs. Torches used to light a path, and light the readings in the days before electricity. They were practical. Like a Light spell. Now, they symbolize the Light of Christ made present in our midst.

Cross

It's hard to live in a Christian country and not know what the cross is. But why do Episcopalians carry one around all the time, at the head of every procession? As a people of embodied faith, we need to see the symbol, which we follow. We need to be reminded of the means of our salvation. We need to practice following Jesus on the cross in worship so that we remember to follow him in the world. The cross may or may not be a *crucifix*; that is, a cross that includes the suffering Christ. Traditional vampire mythology has held that crucifixes and *not* crosses repel vampires, but the Buffyverse holds that they are equally effective.

Chalice

The cup of the carpenter, which must be chosen wisely.[1] This chalice is the vessel that holds the blood of Christ. Usually, you'll see silver chalices in Episcopal churches, because silver has anti-microbial properties. It's a good thing to have when you share a common cup. Not to mention that it shows up as the Chalice of Destiny, marking the value of that which it holds. But some churches prefer to go with a more simple cup, one more like that which Jesus might have actually used at the Last Supper. So sometimes it's a clay cup. Either way, it is the cup of salvation.

Paten

Fancy word for plate. It holds the *priest's host,* the big wafer that gets broken at the end of the Eucharistic Prayer. It usually matches the chalice—if the chalice is silver, the paten is silver. If the chalice is terra cotta, the paten is terra cotta. It fits snugly in the chalice when part of the *stack,* the pile of chalice, purificator, paten, pall, veil, and burse.

Purificator

A linen napkin used to wipe the chalice between each use. It's starched stiffly and folded into thirds, for the Trinity.

Pall

The stiff card that protects the veil from crumbs of the *host.* It sits on top of the paten to help the veil keep its shape, and is usually embroidered with a holy symbol—a cross, or maybe a Chi Rho, or the Lamb Victorious.

Veil

A beautiful, silken veil covers the stack, veiling the elements from sight. It always matches the liturgical color of the day. Like the *corporal,* it is folded into ninths, then laid in such a way that the front makes a pyramid.

Burse

A burse is basically a flat purse that rests on top of the veil. It also matches the liturgical color of the day. The *corporal* usually rests inside the burse until it is carefully laid out on the altar for the Eucharist. The tabernacle key is also usually found inside. It's basically a treasure chest made out of fabric.

Fair Linen

A clean, white cloth laid over the altar to protect both the altar and the eucharistic elements from one another. The fair linen is like what might protect your eyes when the Ark of the Covenant is opened. The eucharistic elements are all prevented from touching the altar, crumbs are taken care of—it protects everything.

Altar Book

The giant, ancient-looking book containing the Chant of Eucharist. Every priest needs an altar book in order to chant (or say—if that's your bag) the Eucharistic Prayer. There are eight possible prayers, all of which can be spoken, sung on Simple Tone (which, ironically, is by far the most challenging option), or sung on Solemn Tone. Other parts of the service are included, but the priest usually uses the Book of Common Prayer for those parts.

Cruet

A very small pitcher, usually silver, pewter, or glass, that holds water or wine for use in the Eucharist.

Flagon

A very large pitcher made of silver, pewter, or glass that holds water or wine for use in the Eucharist.

Lavabo Bowl and Towel

Lavabo comes from the Latin word for "to clean." During the Offertory, an acolyte washes the presider's hands while she prays, "Create in me a clean heart, O God, and renew a right spirit within me"[2] silently. The acolyte pours water from a cruet over the priest's hands into the lavabo bowl, then offers the towel so she can dry her hands before the Eucharist. It's a ritual, more cleansing of the heart than the hands. It reminds everyone present of the Collect for Purity: "Cleanse the thoughts of our hearts"—and our hands.

Corporal

A large square of white linen, folded into ninths, usually with a cross in the bottom middle square. Like *Hollywood Squares*. The corporal is folded up and placed in the burse for the bulk of the service, then is taken out and carefully unfolded during the Offertory to prepare the Table for what is about to happen. After the Eucharist, it is carefully folded inward to prevent crumbs from falling to the floor.

Tabernacle

A small cabinet usually mounted on the wall near the altar as a safe place to reserve extra consecrated bread and wine. If this cabinet is recessed into the wall, it's called an *aumbry*. Just for kicks. Because we needed more special words. Episcopalians believe that Christ is Really Present in some mystical way in the bread and wine, so some Episcopalians kneel before the tabernacle in reverence.

Sanctuary Lamp

The sanctuary lamp burns before the tabernacle 24/7, to make sure all who pass by know that they are in the presence of something holy. This tradition comes to us from the ever-burning fire that Samuel tended in the Temple. Jewish synagogues continue to have a light that stands before its tabernacle, which contains the Torah. In Episcopal churches, the lamp is only put out once a year, on Maundy Thursday (or Good Friday, if the consecrated elements are reserved for Holy Communion from the Reserved Sacrament that day) when all the bread is consumed and no new bread can be consecrated until Easter.

So we've got all this equipment. Now, where to use them? Even the physical building—the church—has names associated with its nooks and crannies.

Narthex

What in other buildings would be known only as a foyer is known in the church as the narthex. It is the first room you encounter when you enter the West Door. This is where all the ministers and acolytes line up before the service, where the ushers hand out the service bulletins, where the nametags are kept. Fancy name, ordinary place.

Like Aslan coming from over the sea, Christians believe that Jesus, our Light, our Lamp, our Sun, will return from the east. So our churches "face" east, which means the altar is at the eastern end. That's right, it's not just Muslims who face east (at least in the United States) to pray. The main entrance, then, would be in the west. Sometimes, because of the needs of the site (or, for example, if a church is worshipping in a place that wasn't originally built to be a place of worship), the altar cannot be at the east end. So we've developed the concept of "liturgical east," which basically means "towards the altar." So we would call the primary entrance the West Door, even if one enters from the south.

Nave

The main part of the church where the congregation sits. Historically, churches were cross-shaped. Even modern churches, which tend to omit the *transepts*, tend to be long rectangles leading from the West Door to the High Altar. The nave is that space in between. The word comes from the Latin for "ship" (think navy), and if you look up, many churches' ceilings give the impression that we are worshipping in an upturned boat.

Transepts

The "arms" of the cross-shape in the church. Worshippers who sit in these *pews* typically face the altar from the side.

Pews

Y'all know what church benches are called. Don't front.

Quire

The section at the front of the church where the choir sits. In historic Anglican tradition, the choir is divided into two sides, *cantoris* and *decani*, with the main aisle between them. It is situated between the *nave*, where the congregation sits, and the *sanctuary*, where the altar is held. Choirs can also sit in a *gallery*, which can be anywhere convenient in the church building. I have no idea why we spell it "quire" instead of "choir." but isn't it cool?

I also have no idea why many Episcopalians pronounce the Latin canticle *Venite* (ven-ee-teh) as "ven-ai-tee" but, as Mallory Ortberg always says, life is a rich and varied tapestry.

Lectern

The reading stand from which lessons from the Old and New Testament are read. *Pews* on this side of the aisle are said to be on the "Epistle" side, because many of the New Testament readings are from the epistles. Sometimes the lectern is in the shape of an eagle on whose outstretched wings the Bible rests. The Word of God flies forth into the world.

Pulpit

The raised reading stand from which the Gospel is preached. It typically is grander and more magnificent than the lectern, to signify the primacy of the Gospel. *Pews* on this side of the aisle are said to be on the "Gospel" side. Both the *pulpit* and the *lectern* are in the nave section of the church.

> I have been in churches that *insisted* that stage right was the Gospel side. I have been in churches that *insisted* that stage left was the Gospel side. I usually just go with "the side the pulpit is on," though historically it is liturgical north (stage right).

Sanctuary

The easternmost part of the church, which houses the *altar*. Non-Episcopal churches usually use this word to refer to the *nave*, or to the entire worship space, so sometimes you'll hear that in Episcopal churches, too. It's not quite as precise as I usually like to be though, so stick with using it for the *altar* section.

Altar rail

The rail that divides the *sanctuary* from the quire, where communicants may kneel to receive the sacrament of Holy Communion.

Sedilia

A seat, usually recessed into the wall, for the *celebrant* and other ministers who need to be seated in the *sanctuary*. Often very grand, with decorated arches overhead, at least in older churches.

Altar

The Holy Table, upon which sacrifices of praise and thanksgiving are offered unto almighty God. May be against the wall, necessitating an east-facing celebration of the Eucharist, or out from the wall, offering the celebrant the choice to face *ad orientem* or *versus populi*.

Ad orientem vs. versus populi. These are just the Latin for "east-facing" and "toward the people." Back when all the altars were against the east wall, the celebrant faced toward the people for certain parts, and toward the altar for others. Now it is much more common for celebrants to stand behind the altar and face the people for the entire celebration. There are merits to east-facing worship, though. The priest, instead of standing in Christ's place as the host, stands as lead worshipper, addressing God and leading the people as we all face God as one. The east wall acts as a sort of veil between earth and heaven in this scenario. *Ad orientem* Eucharists are less common than those celebrated *versus populi* for all sorts of reasons, but a church geek should be familiar with both possibilities.

The Adventure Path
Let's Go to Church

In which the adventurer attends Sunday worship

 [This chapter is pretty essential. Make sure you've read up on all the "Equipment" (page 79), "Vestments" (page 72), and "The Player's Handbook" (page 21) before you dive in to this encounter.]

You walk into an Episcopal church on a Sunday morning. The sunlight filters in through brightly colored stained glass windows, spilling beams of copper, gold, and aqua over the rich dark wood of the pews. The solid heels of your shoes click on the hard slate floor as you take a service leaflet and walk down the center aisle to a pew of your choice. As you genuflect before the altar before taking your seat, you can feel the air around you, heavy with the scent of incense, pregnant with the weight of generations of prayers that have been said in this space. The stones radiate these prayers, prayers they have held for decades, prayers they remember long after those who prayed them have died. You gently let down the kneeler in front of you, trying not to let it thud as it hits the floor.

Genuflection is a quick drop to one knee, indicating honor for that which one is genuflecting towards. It is traditional to genuflect before a tabernacle containing the consecrated Host, though some will do so before any sanctified altar. Some people cross themselves as they genuflect, but that is by no means universal. A customary act in the Middle Ages, it is a show of respect for a king or noble was demonstrated by going down on one knee, often remaining there until told to rise. Other than at Ren Faires, you've probably only seen genuflection used when making a proposal of marriage.

All around you are people getting ready for the service—in silent prayer, in greeting friends they haven't seen in a long time, in helping children with their "busy bags" and coloring books, as they prepare to worship Almighty God. The *Christus Rex*—Christ the King, Christ the Triumphant—looms over the congregation, benevolently presiding over all this preparation. He is already here. His presence fills the room, as tactile as mist, washing over people who back in the parking lot were not nearly so cheerful, not nearly so generous, not nearly so reverent.

Churches differ when it comes to their **display of the cross**. Many Episcopal churches have a crucifix, on which hangs the suffering Christ, the savior of the world. Others have an empty cross, which signifies that Christ is resurrected and the cross is now empty. And some churches have what is called a *Christus Rex*, a cross which Jesus is present, but past his suffering. He may be robed in white (or in a chasuble, like the priest below), and is often wearing a crown.

The Procession

There is a rustle at the back of the church. Turning your head surreptitiously as you pretend to continue your prayers, you can see the **crucifer** and **acolytes** getting into place. The organist begins the **prelude**, and you sink back into eternity as your prayers rise before the Lord like incense. Stand as the **processional hymn** begins—you might hear a **sacring bell** rung to let you know it's time—and pull out a well-worn copy of the faded blue Hymnal 1982 to join in singing the opening hymn.

Row upon row of ministers march past, calling your mind to old military processions, really the only other institution to move forward with such pomp and ceremony. You are alerted to their advent by the **thurifer's** approach, swinging a smoking pot of incense as he processes up the aisle, letting people know that all those who follow him are holy, set apart, dedicated to the Lord. The **cross** is just behind, flanked by two **torches** that symbolize the light of Christ. The **choir** follows, their voices swelling the song of the congregation, adding harmony and bolstering your praise. Another cross follows, leading the **lector** and **chalice bearers** to their places. (Assuming this is the practice in your congregation, of course.)

Behind them come the **clergy**, their **cassocks** and **surplices** swishing around their feet as they process forward into the community. The sacred ministers (or altar ministers, or guys with the Best Outfits) bring up the rear. First the **subdeacon**, then the **deacon**, and then the **presider**, whether **bishop** or **priest**. This morning, no bishop is present. The priest, smilingly jovial in her **chasuble**, sings out lustily as she passes you through the aisle. She presses on down the aisle, pausing at the **font** to dip her hand into the water, spraying droplets down her front as she makes the sign of the cross, remembering her baptism, purifying her heart as she approaches the altar of God.

The Word of God

As the hymn ends, she turns to face you. In the ancient chanting tone, she greets you with, "Blessed be God: Father, Son, and Holy

Spirit." You reply, "And blessed be His kingdom, now and forever. Amen." With the chant, more so than anything else, you feel transported to a realm that is out-of-time. This place is not like any other. You behave in a way that's different than anywhere else. It looks like the end of *A New Hope* and sounds like the monks from *Monty Python and the Holy Grail*. Your Wis bonus goes up as you experience the ancient ways of moving, of being, and you encounter parts of yourself you had forgotten existed.

Why do we use so much Latin and Greek? Greek was, in many ways, the first language of the church. Most of the New Testament is written in Greek, and most early followers of Jesus spoke Greek to one another. As the Gospel spread westward, and especially after Christianity became the religion of the Roman Empire in the early 300s, Latin came into common use as well. In fact, Roman Catholic Masses were nearly always said in Latin until the 1960s. Even though the Episcopal Church has used the *vernacular* (that is, the native language of the locals) in worship for a very long time, we often still title our *canticles* (songs and poems) with their Latin or Greek names. Look at the Psalms in the prayer book—they all have a Latin title. This practice connects us with our history and reminds us that we are only the keepers, not the owners, of the traditions of the worship of God. We do not have the authority to compel or prohibit worship; we are merely Stewards of Gondor, remaining faithful until such time as the King shall return.

Where you go next on your adventure depends on the season of the church year. There is always a song (or, if the Mass is *spoken*, it could be what I like to call communal slam poetry) next that sets the tone for the service. In most seasons, you will sing "Glory to God in the highest," praising God in tones that soar to the firmament. Because Latin is our jam, we call this the **Gloria.** In more penitential times, worship begins with "Kyrie eleison," usually shortened in title to the **Kyrie.** This is what Hollywood thinks "church music" sounds like. In the background of most church scenes, someone is singing "Kyrie eleison" in the background. In Westeros, this would be the score for the scene where Cersei makes her penance walk. It's Greek for "Lord have mercy," and reminds us that, in this season, the primary purpose of our worship is to ask for God's mercy. You are less likely to hear the **Trisagion,** or "thrice-holy," in which we proclaim our awe and wonder at the mightiness and holiness of God.

As the last notes of the community's song die away, the presider's voice rings out alone, "The Lord be with you." You respond, "So say we all" (just kidding). The actual response is, "And also with you," and there is a short time of silence for you to offer your prayers. The priest collects those prayers as she turns to God and prays the **Collect of the Day**. Your "Amen" affirms her prayer, and then, in quiet unison (or slightly more noisy unison, depending on how many children are in attendance), the congregation sits for the reading of the **Lessons**. The **lector** steps to the **lectern** and thunders out, "A reading from the book of Isaiah," in tones reminiscent of a Monty Python character intoning "Blessed are the cheese makers." You stifle your giggles in order to hear the Word of the Lord as spoken to Isaiah the prophet, and then pray the **Psalm** with the choir. The **subdeacon** (or another lector) stands, reverences the **altar,** and moves to the lectern to read the **Epistle** as the community continues to pray. As the chords of the Anglican chant wash over you, your gaze takes in the child coloring in front of you, the couple chanting their Psalm from their iPads, and the person sneaking in late and hoping no one notices.

The man at the end of the row's head nods ever closer to his chest as the **subdeacon** continues to read, then snaps up as the man awakes with a start at the opening strains of the **sequence hymn**. You collect your hymnal and stand to sing as the procession moves to the center of the aisle, turning in place to face the altar party as they proceed. You want to keep your eye on the Gospel, just as ancient listeners' eyes sought Jesus. The cross is lifted high over the community, soaring, as though it were meant to represent the Holy Spirit as a dove, rather than Jesus's crucifixion. It stops rather suddenly, as the **crucifer** suddenly remembers the acolyte master's admonition, "No spinning Jesus." The **subdeacon** steps into place before the cross, between the two torches, and holds out her hands for the **Gospel**

Book. A flash of color whips by as the **Gospeller** opens the jeweled cover and finds his place. He hands the golden-drenched book to the **subdeacon** and turns to the **thurifer**, bowing. As the hymn dies away, he swings the fragrant pot over the book three times, chanting "The Holy Gospel of our Lord Jesus Christ according to Luke." You hastily drop your hymnal to cross yourself at forehead, lips, and heart, in the ancient gesture of prayer, asking God to keep these holy words in your head, on your lips, and in your heart. The **Gospeller** returns the smoking **thurible** to the **thurifer** as you chant back, "Glory to you, Lord Christ," bowing in your turn.

Standing in the midst of the crowd, the **Gospeller** reads out the lesson appointed for the day. You wonder if this is what it felt like to hear Jesus in his day, as you stand on tiptoe to catch a glimpse of the Gospel party over the shoulder of the insufferably tall person next to you. Just before you trip over your Chucks into him, the Gospeller suddenly concludes with "The Gospel of the Lord," and you manage to gasp out "Praise to you, Lord Christ" and swing your hymnal back into place without anyone noticing. The Gospel party processes back to the **altar** as you finish your hymn. The **preacher** stands ready at the **pulpit**, and it's time for the **sermon**.

The sermon, bless its heart, is one of the most maligned parts of the service. Everyone has a story about the worst sermon they've ever heard. Take a second and think of yours. I'll wait.

Now that your jokes and complaints and whininess about the whole entire concept of a sermon are out of the way, let's talk about what a good sermon looks like. A good sermon explains. A good sermon inspires. A good sermon challenges. A good sermon uplifts. A good sermon makes you want to shout "Amen!" Or maybe it makes you want to talk it over at lunch with your friends. Or even get out your Bible at home and look at the passage again. Now, no preacher can do this every single Sunday. Maybe the Reverend Dr. Martin Luther King Jr. could, but you probably don't go to Dr. King's church. And preachers have off days. So if you hear a bad sermon, don't completely write off this church as not worth your time. On the other hand, don't subject yourself to a year of bad sermons.

Good preaching is the bedrock of an engaged, well-informed, well-supported congregation, and you deserve to hear it.

In the Episcopal Church, most sermons are going to be short. Fifteen minutes, max. Episcopalians are not like our evangelical brethren and sistren who parse one verse of Ephesians for forty-five minutes. Neither are we like our friends in the Baptist tradition, who weave in Scriptures not from the lessons to make a general point that encompasses the vast majority of the worship time. Episcopalians, most of the time, make one point—just one, to help the congregation see what God is doing in the lessons appointed for the day, and to imagine how God might be doing something similar right now.

Sometimes we might make this point with humor, other times with a good story. We might make a point that comforts you in times of sorrow, and we might make a point that challenges you to confront the sin in your life, and to love God and your neighbor a little better in the future. As we've already discussed, the lessons are appointed on a three-year cycle, so if you come back three years later, you'll hear the same lessons again. But the sermon will almost certainly be different. The Holy Scriptures contain so much, that it is impossible, in a ten or fifteen minute talk, to capture every single thing that God is doing in that story.

Take the Parable of the Prodigal Son (Luke 15:11–32), for example. Most people know that one. Father has two sons, one takes his share of the inheritance, runs off, squanders it, comes back, father forgives him and gives him more than he even asked for, other son resentful. Remember now? So the most common reading of this parable is that the father is God, the prodigal (wasteful) son is humankind, God forgives us when we sin. But then preachers put on different emphases. Is it more important that the son returned home, or that the father went out to meet him before he even apologized? And what about the older son? Does he represent judgmental churchy types who resent those undeserving types who are forgiven and welcomed into the fold "too easily"? We could hear a sermon from the father's perspective, from either of the sons— heck, even the fatted calf could tell her story. What do you need to hear in this parable? Chances are, someone else needs to hear something different. And over the course of a lifetime in church, you will hear, every three years, a new way of thinking, a new way of connecting, a new way of seeing what God does in the story of God's relationships with humankind. And all of those ways will matter to someone. So, just 'cause it wasn't what *you* needed to hear today, doesn't mean it wasn't important. Can I get an amen?

The Creed and the Prayers

Now that you've done been preached to, you shake your limbs awake to stand for the **Nicene Creed.** While the sermon changes every week, the Creed always stays the same. This ancient witness to our three-fold God has been the foundation of our faith since the 380s, and its repetition in worship roots us with the confessions of those who came before us. We believe what they believed, and we stand here today because of their witness to God's power and God's mercy. We speak the words, as one community, unified not in some kind of hegemonic, faceless oneness, drones reciting the Oath to the Capitol out of fear of retribution.[1] No, we are unified organically—one body with many members, one plant rooted in Christ with many branches, one tree that anchors the whole swamp, allowing us to find and support those who are lost. In our unity, our diversity is not lost; rather our diversity informs our unity, adding new bands of light to the prism of our faith.

Sometimes people struggle with this idea of "**We believe.**" "What if I don't believe that?" they ask me. "What if I'm not sure?" Here's the important thing: In the Episcopal Church, we believe in *common* prayer—that is, the prayer of the community. So it's not so important what you believe. The community believes it. And if you're struggling with part of it—the resurrection of the dead after a loss, the forgiveness of sins after someone has hurt you— then let the community believe that, pray that, for you until you are ready to believe it again. The Creed is the healer in the party, the one who helps carry you when your Con is low.

Anchored in this historic community, we are empowered to make the **Prayers of the People.** While the forms differ from rite to rite, from church to church, from season to season, prayer is always offered with intercession for:

The Universal Church, its members, and its mission

Remember that organic unity from the last paragraph? It doesn't happen just by accident. It happens through centuries of prayer and work; generations of conscious decision that it is better to worship God together than apart. Whether we feel the Church is living out its mission faithfully or that it is failing miserably, it needs our prayers.

The Nation and all in authority

Ditto here. It is my contention that our increased partisan polarization would be slowed if, each and every Sunday, we prayed for those in authority—even those we didn't vote for; *especially* those we didn't vote for. As I write this, my home parish prays daily for a Democrat and two Republicans as we ask God's blessing on our president, governor, and mayor. Hardly anyone in the parish voted for all three of them, nor does any one person approve of the work all three of them are doing. Lord knows that sometimes I pray for God to whack one of them upside the head and take them in a totally new direction. But our prayers acknowledge the legitimacy and the reality of their authority and make it harder for us to demonize them or think of them as somehow monstrous, inhuman. We pray for those in authority because the Bible tells us to (1 Timothy 2:2), and because they bear responsibility for many, many lives, whether we wish that were true or not.

The welfare of the world

This is the trickiest proposition for those coming from a skeptical background. Praying for the welfare of the world is no substitute for working for the welfare of the world. But prayer is work, and work is prayer. We pray for God to help us improve the welfare of the world that it may live into the reality that God has envisioned.

The concerns of the local community

These are the prayers most of us are the most familiar with. The prayers close to our hearts, as we unburden our souls to God, asking for God's blessing on our aunt with cancer, and our neighbor who just lost their job, our best friend who just had a miscarriage, and for discernment as we decide whether this boyfriend is "The One." These prayers are also the most mockable—the ones we often abuse by praying for our favorite Sports Team™, or that we might roll a natural 20. But while God might not care who wins the Super Bowl (sorry, y'all), God does care to hear the deepest pleas of our hearts, and to walk alongside us, even if the outcome does not change.

Those who suffer and those in any trouble

Here we continue the petitionary payers begun above, but we remember those we do not know who are suffering. These prayers, like those for the welfare of the world, spur us to action, and encourage us to think about why we don't know anyone who's suffering in that way, and how we might ease the suffering of others.

The departed

Why do we pray for the departed? Are we praying to get their soul out of Purgatory faster? "As soon as the prayer in the churchyard rings, the soul from Purgatory springs"[2] style? Or maybe we're praying against undead? #WellActually . . . we pray for the dead as we pray for the living. In the Episcopal Church, we don't believe that whatever state you're in when you die determines your eternal place. The Final Judgment won't happen until Jesus's Second Coming, which time we do not know the day or the hour. Death parts us from our loved ones, but it does not relieve us of the responsibility of praying for them. We pray that they might grow in the knowledge and love of God, that they might go from strength to strength in the life of perfect service to God's heavenly kingdom. Just as we prayed for them in life, we pray for them in death.

Phew. That's a lot of groups to pray for. But it's important to have guidelines, otherwise we would only pray for the other characters in the party, or for items that make the news, or (worst of all) for our own needs. We would turn God into some grand Cosmic Butler, a great genie offering wishes and turning us into princes, rather than properly petitioning the King of the universe for the things we have been told to ask for. But there are other types of prayer than intercession and petition, particularly the **Confession**, which we move to next.

The Confession and Absolution of Sins

If you're anything like me, the Creed and the Prayers of the People are where you start to nod off. All that standing and speaking in unison starts to run together for me. I'm sure it's different for everybody—somebody's got to like *The Phantom Menace*. But I always love the feeling of kicking the bright-colored kneeler down, and hearing those pages flip as the congregation drops to their knees for the Confession.

The concept of sin has been a controversial one in the Church for the last several decades. "Fire and brimstone" preaching is mentioned with disdain. "Bible thumpers" have become "Bible beaters"—beating those they don't like about the head with their favorite verses. And who likes thinking about sin, anyway? We like to think of ourselves as lovable rogues who may have shot first, but hey, we've got a heart of gold. Here's the thing: the General Confession, which we all say together without singling any one person (or one sin) out, definitely expresses that we are capable of great things. But we also screw up. We don't always love God with our whole heart. We don't always love our neighbors as ourselves. Even if we're Lawful Good, we are supremely capable of rationalizing our actions in such a way that we always come out the Good Guys. And so the

Confession is an opportunity for us to acknowledge that being good doesn't mean we have to be perfect.

After the Confession, the priest stands and offers the **Absolution**, making the sign of the cross over the people: "Almighty God have mercy on you, forgive you all your sins through our Lord Jesus Christ, strengthen you in all goodness, and by the power of the Holy Spirit keep you in eternal life."[3]

You feel as though a literal weight has been lifted as you rise from your knees, leaving little impressions in the kneeler pad to show where you've been. But now your sins have been lifted, like a curse has been removed. You drank the antitoxin, and the poison is leeched out of your body—at least for a time.

Your newfound freedom unlocks a new feat for you: the Peace of the Lord. You receive the **Peace** via the priest, and share it with your pew-neighbors with a handshake, or a hug, or maybe a wave. At some churches, this ritual is long and complex, requiring each and every person to greet each and every other person in the congregation. At others, you might receive nothing more than a handshake from your nearest neighbor and a nod from his neighbor before the priest moves on to the **Offertory**.

The Holy Communion

The Peace and the Offertory together serve as the hinge that turns the service from the **Ministry of the Word** to the **Holy Communion.** The priest invites you to offer yourself, your soul and body, to Almighty God, then begins to prepare the holy altar for the central rite of worship. Dark-suited ushers silently pass a burnished brass plate from row to row to the rich sounds of organ music. After casually tossing your offering to God in the plate—it's very weird how casual we are about this, by the way, because it's kind of a big deal—you allow the music to drift over you, taking you almost into a meditative state to prepare your heart and mind to be caught up into the Divine Liturgy, the Holy Communion, the Everlasting Feast that is going on forever and ever in heaven, and whose stream we are able to dip a toe into for just a moment, though the impact is as intense as stepping into the Wardrobe.

This is the point in the Adventure Path when it gets real. The first half of the worship, we have been praising God, to be sure, but we have mostly been sharing the story of God with God's people, exploring the best way to live in God's world, declaring our belief in God's goodness, and asking God's mercy on us, and on those whom we love in the world. So while there's certainly been some talking to God, it's been more focused on talking about God. But now it is time for the Holy Communion. Communion with God, wherein we directly thank God, we remember what Christ has done, we invoke the presence of the Holy Spirit, we commune with God, taking him into our very selves, and we prefigure the great banquet in heaven, where all feast in abundance greater even than that seen at Redwall Abbey.

You stand as the **offering plates** are processed past you, sometimes following the cross. The priest accepts the plates, as well as bread and wine, and presents the offerings to God. You wonder if fire has ever descended from heaven to sanctify the gifts, so solemnly and carefully does the priest lift the plates on high. She makes the sign of the cross over them, a symbol of blessing that marks them as Christ's. She reverently pours wine into the chalice, mingling a small amount of water with it to remember that Christ, in his Incarnation, mingled divinity with humanity. The Holy Table is set, the **corporal** laid out on top of the **fair linen**, the **chalice** and **paten** set out, the **Altar Book** is opened, and the **acolyte** ritually washes the priest's hands.

The *orans* **position** is an ancient prayer posture of arms outstretched and slightly raised. [See the panel by chasuble on page 76.] We have paintings of Christians praying in this way from first-century Rome.

She steps behind the **altar** and spreads her hands open to make the *orans* **position.** This ancient prayer posture evokes the image of welcome, of hospitality, and of openness to God. She begins the ancient chant called in Latin, *Sursum corda,* "Lift up your hearts." You respond to her call in unison with the rest of the congregation. The chant wafts over you, filling the space with the sound of the holy, rising tangibly through the air like incense. She praises God for God's mighty actions in Creation, in the Incarnation, Crucifixion, and Resurrection of Jesus Christ, and in God's continued providence through the abiding presence of the Holy Spirit. Her praise matches the theological theme of the season: If you are attending worship during Lent, she thanks God for the incredible mercy we have received through the forgiveness of our sins. If you are attending worship during the Christmas season, she thanks God that Jesus was made a perfect Man of the flesh of the Virgin Mary, his mother.

You are jolted out of your reverie as the priest cues you it is time to sing the **Sanctus.** The whole congregation sings the ancient song from Isaiah's vision of the Seraphim—giant creatures with six wings. As they fly around (covering their faces? And feet?) they sing, "Holy, holy, holy is the Lord of Hosts; the whole earth is full of his glory."[4] You sing this hymn, calling all those seraphs, and the saints who have gone before us, and all the company of heaven to join this earthly congregation as you worship. Think of the celebration at the end of *Return of the Jedi* in the Special Edition (I know, I know). It's not just the Ewoks celebrating, it's not even just the entire star system celebrating, it includes everyone, even those who died before the victory was assured.

After the Sanctus, the congregation kneels (or continues standing, depending on their piety), as the priest stops chanting to remind you of the story of salvation. She recounts God's continued attempts to get our attention and show us a better way to live, and our history of ignoring those attempts. The heart of the story recounts the Last Supper. How on the night before he died, Jesus was at supper with his friends. At this ordinary meal, he took bread, gave thanks, and broke it, and told those friends that it was his body, making this everyday meal holy. They continued with the meal, and at the end of it Jesus took a common cup that held wine, said the blessing, and shared it among them all, telling them that it was his blood. The words surrounding the story have changed over the years, adapting to different cultural contexts and emphasizing different pieces, but those central words, the ones that Jesus said, have stayed the same since they were first included in Paul's first letter to the Corinthian church, in about 45 CE. They're solid, foundational. They are the words that show us the food at the Never-Feast. They are the words that show us "Truuuuueeee Loooooovvveee." You notice some in the congregation bowing their heads as these words are spoken to show reverence and awe.

The priest concludes the prayer by making the sign of the cross with the bread over the cup as she invokes the name of Jesus, then encircling the cup as she prays, "in the unity of the Holy Spirit." In so doing, she binds up the prayer of the congregation in the strong name of the Trinity, invoking its power to make Christ Really Present. She bows deeply as the congregation responds with the Great Amen to acknowledge this as the heart of your worship.

As she rises, the congregation joins her in chanting the Lord's Prayer, the one that Jesus himself taught. It, too, has remained (mostly) unchanged since first recorded in the Gospels of Matthew and Luke. The prayer concludes, and she lifts the bread high in the air, peering almost *through* it—as though by looking so intently, she can see through the bread and perceive the presence of Christ (h/t to Jamie Fraser of *Outlander* fame for the illustration). A crack thunders through the nave, louder than breaking a cracker has any right to be. You tremble as you wait through the silence that marks the memory of Christ's broken body. "Alleluia!" the priest calls out, "Christ our Passover has been sacrificed for us." You gratefully respond, "Therefore, let us keep the feast." The organ begins to hum softly as the altar servers move forward so that the business of receiving communion can begin.

The church rustles as everyone stirs from the stillness that came from participating in the most holy Eucharist. Your neighbors let their coughs out, bulletins get shuffled, and children start their murmuring back up. You watch as the ushers solemnly step back, indicating that its time for each pew to step forward to receive communion. Your knees creak as you reverence the altar on your way up—literally. Most churches include stairs as you ascend toward the Most High, their architecture indicating the supremacy of God's holy altar. Flecks of water brush your face as the child in front of you splashily dips his fingers into the font to bless himself on his way to the altar. You hurriedly copy his gesture, furtively watching everyone else to make sure you're doing it right. You are. You sink to your knees on the soft, needlepoint cushion in between an immaculately haberdashed elderly woman and a young man in cargo shorts. They make the sign of the cross, almost in unison.

The priest makes her way down the row, offering bread to **communicants** and blessings to those who have yet to be baptized. Be-cassocked **servers** hurry to follow her, the skirts of their vestments whooshing as they walk past. The devotion on display is breathtaking. To witness such faithfulness, such devotion moves you to your core. These sages—not only those serving communion but those receiving—have been seeking reconciliation with God and one another for decades. The priest presses the bread into your hand—hard. Though it's only a light cracker or morsel of bread, it feels heavy enough to carry the sin of the world.

You swallow the wafer, then tip the **chalice** towards you as the server tilts it for you. The cool silver touches your lips, then a rush of warm red wine floods over the edge. As you tip it back towards the server, the light glows gold as it reflects back from the chalice, evoking the presence of Christ. The server wipes the rim with the **purificator** as you cross yourself and rise to head back to your seat. You kneel in your pew in reverence for the continued communion between heaven and earth taking place at the altar rail. You avert your eyes as a priest swishes past to offer communion to an elderly woman sitting in a wheelchair at the end of your row. As the music fades, the celebrant steps behind the altar to begin the **Post-Communion Prayer**.

Your reverie continues as you thank God for the gift of Christ's presence in the Holy Communion, but you begin to stir during the

"Amens." The priest raises her hand in blessing, chanting, "The peace of God which passes all understanding keep your hearts and minds in the knowledge and love of God, and of his Son Jesus Christ our Lord. And the blessing of God Almighty: the Father, the Son, and the Holy Spirit be amongst you and remain with you always. Amen."[5]

The Recessional

The kneelers clunk back into place, the organ kicks into high gear, the congregation stands, and the acolytes grab their equipment to begin the retiring procession. You flip your hymnal open to the concluding hymn as the organ groans through its introduction. Its trumpets blare like the end of *A New Hope*. You bow as the crucifer walks past, then catch the eye of one of the assisting priests as he gets a *little* too into the song. The other assisting priest is waving to a toddler two rows ahead of you. The celebrant tries to glare at them but can't keep herself in a bad mood. She fist bumps you, then books it to the back as the hymn draws to a close. The deacon, if there is one, dismisses the community with a hearty, "Let us go forth in the name of Christ!" then hands his prayer book to the subdeacon so he can greet the congregation as they walk out.

You gather your things, reverence the altar, then head forth into the world, refreshed for another week. You glance up at the "Work is Prayer" sign over the exit as you leave and prepare your heart for a week serving Christ in the world. Roll initiative!

Comic-Con Lite
The General Convention

Which takes place in the room where it happens

 [This chapter is for wonks who enjoy church legislation and political intrigue. If you've instead got a "pleasing expectation of retreat"[1] from all that, skip to "Magic" on page 119 for a primer on the basic theological stances of The Episcopal Church.]

Welcome to the original Gen Con. General Convention goes back all the way to 1789, and while there's way less role-playing, this is the con that invented geektastic fun. You want Cabinet Battles, à la Jefferson and Hamilton? Got 'em. You want an exhibition hall filled with free swag and celebrities with whom to take selfies? Got 'em. You want beautiful worship every day that celebrates the diversity of the church? Got it. General Convention meets every three years in cities all around the United States. It's one part con, one part congress, and one part family reunion. If you're an Episco-nerd, it's basically heaven for ten days (sometimes in Iowa).[2]

This chapter is less for your traditional geek, and more for the wonks. Wonks are political geeks. They're like us, only instead of arguing about the size and configuration of the *Galactica* or whether Han shot first, they argue about whether tax cuts grow the economy and whether increasing background checks decreases gun violence. And Episcopal wonks care about the canons. Millions of Episcopalians go their whole lives without ever even thinking about General Convention, much less going to one. But if wonkery is your game, settle in for an introduction to the greatest, churchiest, wonkiest ten days in existence.

The Constitution and Canons of the Episcopal Church are our primary governing and legal documents. They lay out who we are, what we do, who can do what, and how it all gets done. Changing them isn't *quite* as difficult as amending the U.S. Constitution, but it's close.

A History of the Episcopal Church (Abridged)

You know that guy who modulates the key but won't debate with Hamilton? The one who says the U.S. Congress doesn't speak for him? Yeah, that's Samuel Seabury, the first bishop of the Episcopal Church. He was a Loyalist priest during the Revolutionary War, but afterward decided to stay and continue to preach Good News in the Anglican tradition to this new republic. But there were no bishops here (England had never allowed the New World to have their own bishop), so no way to confirm adult believers and no way to ordain new priests. No way to govern whole areas of churches together.

So Samuel Seabury took matters into his own hands. He sailed to England and asked to be ordained bishop, *sans* the loyalty oath to King George that bishops had to take. When the English bishops said "No, thanks," Samuel Seabury remained undeterred. He rode north to Scotland, where they were rather more sympathetic to his desire to avoid swearing loyalty to King Geordie, and got himself ordained bishop of Connecticut, the first (and for a while, only) bishop in the Protestant Episcopal Church of the United States of America.

As you can imagine, Bishop Seabury cared a great deal about the authority of bishops, and the necessity of having bishops in order for the church to go on. Other founders of the Episcopal Church were less . . . reliant on bishops for the survival of the church's mission. William White, who had been chaplain to the Second Continental Congress (that'd be the one that wrote the Declaration of Independence), felt that while bishops were useful, their absence did not represent a crisis for this new expression of Anglicanism. White viewed the Revolution as an opportunity to create a more democratic form of governance, not unlike that of this new nation, and in 1785 (that's right; *before* the first General Convention) set up what he called a House of Deputies. The House of Deputies was comprised of priests and laypersons (all right, lay*men* back in the day), and together, they put together a plan to continue worship in the Anglican tradition in the U.S.

After the ordination of Bishop Seabury, William White and Samuel Provoost also got ordained as bishops, by an English episcopate that was no longer quite so insistent on loyalty oaths as a prerequisite. So they set up a second house (to appease Bishop Seabury, mostly), the House of Bishops. General Convention is the joint meeting of the House of Deputies and the House of Bishops for the purpose of making laws, setting a budget, and reminding ourselves just why we do all of this anyway.

I Was Chosen for the Constitutional Convention

So you're at General Convention. While anyone is welcome to register and attend just for fun, typically, folks at General Convention are vendor / exhibitors, special guests (like ecumenical observers— more on them in a bit), or members of either the House of Bishops or the House of Deputies. All bishops—including retired ones— are members of the House of Bishops, which meets several times a year for fellowship and communication. The House of Bishops feels much more collegial than the House of Deputies, since there are fewer of them and they meet more often. Plus, it's a lifetime appointment. The way in? Get elected bishop (it's not exactly the easiest route). [Check out page 67 for more on the role of a bishop.]

So if you're at General Convention, it's much more likely that you're a deputy. Each diocese elects eight deputies to represent it at General Convention—four clergy (priests and deacons) and four laypersons. Equal representation for all dioceses, no matter their size, wealth, or clout. Like the House of Representatives, deputies must be re-elected before every convention. So there's a lot of turnover, though, like the House of Representatives, there's a fair amount of incumbent inertia. You get more than a few deputies who've been to seven conventions or more. Each diocese also elects four alternate deputies in each order, in case something prevents its deputies from attending, and usually sends at least one clergy and one lay alternate to the actual convention (some dioceses will send all eight). Alternates have no voice or vote on their own, but ten days of legislating can get tiring, so deputies will usually swap out for at least a half-day to relax at some point. So most alternates can plan to spend some time in the House.

So you're there, on the House floor. This is the room where it happens—the art of the trade, how the sausage gets made—though it's rather more transparent than those deals represented in *Hamilton*. While the House of Bishops will occasionally go into executive session and kick all their observers out, their debates are usually public, and the House of Deputies always is. There are over eight hundred deputies, which makes secrecy impractical anyway.

The life of a resolution goes like this: It all starts with an idea. Somebody decides that the Episcopal Church should do something, or take a public position on something, and they get a bishop, a deputy, a standing commission, or a committee to propose a resolution. Each resolution is assigned to a committee (which are organized by topic) and that committee gets to decide what recommendation to make—not usually via rap battles, but the Standing Commission on Liturgy and Music does feature a fair amount of singing. The committee does research and hears testimony from other deputies (and experts) to help make their decision. Committee meetings can drag on a bit, but usually they're where the real interesting stuff happens, in the impassioned testimony of those arguing for or against the resolutions.

Once the committee has decided what to do with the resolution, it makes its way to either the House of Deputies or the House of Bishops (it really doesn't matter which house it starts in, but let's start this one in Deputies, just for ease of reference). The committee chair speechifies for a bit, then the debate is open. Most resolutions are voted on with little discussion, but the controversial ones can inspire debates that last for hours. You can probably guess most of the hotly debated topics, but Episcopalians also tend to get worked up for any resolution that involves changing our worship practices. Sometimes folks will surprise you: Last convention, we argued over where the convention after next should take place for far longer than expected. But once the House has finished debate, it's time to vote.

The Book of Common Prayer is actually part of our constitution. Changing it in any way requires a vote of two consecutive General Conventions. But there are other ways worship can be changed—a new interpretation of the rubrics for worship, for example, or additional saintly commemorations to the calendar. While not nearly so essential as the prayer book itself, these too highlight strains of conflict between Episcopalians and can engender hours of debate.

Most resolutions need simply a voice vote, a vote of acclamation. But if it looks like it's going to be close, the Voting Secretary will manage an electronic vote. An electronic vote allows for some secrecy in voting, an exact count of the votes, and a record of the vote, for posterity. But if it's really for *real* controversial, then someone will call for a "vote by orders" (scare quotes intentional).

I kid, because voting by orders is an important safeguard of our democratic process. But those who know they are on the losing side, but hope that if they try some of what late Supreme Court Justice Scalia would call jiggery-pokery, they might be able to pull a rabbit out of a hat and often use it as a procedural delaying tactic. Voting by orders requires each deputation to divide into its lay half and its clergy half. Each group decides how to vote as a block; each diocese gets one clergy vote and one lay vote. If the deputation cannot agree, their vote counts as "split," which ends up being a "no" in the final tally. Every deputy must sign their name next to their vote to certify it—this one's a big deal.

After all of this, the House can vote to **adopt** the resolution, they can **amend** the resolution and then adopt it, they can **reject** the resolution outright, or they can **send** the resolution back to the committee. The committee hates that last one. But let's say they've adopted our test resolution. Next, the resolution goes to the other House, the House of Bishops, and aaaaalllll that arguing starts over again. There's just one new wrinkle—the House of Bishops must **concur** to the resolution using the exact same language with which it came to them. If they amend it (even to correct the grammar), then it goes back to the House of Deputies again. With only ten legislative days in convention, this sort of legal ping-pong has a limited shelf life; if the two Houses do not concur by the end of convention, the resolution dies for another three years. If the Powers That Be are anxious to do *something* on this topic (or if it's something required, like the budget), the clock becomes a key player in the legislative process, so you'd better write like you're running out of time.

Let's say that for our test resolution, both Houses concur. Congratulations, the Episcopal Church has now officially adopted this resolution. Now, General Convention has in the recent past usually met in the summer (less busy time for churches; cheaper time to book convention halls), and most resolutions don't take effect until the First Sunday of Advent in late November. But the vote of both Houses means that they will take effect once General Convention is over, there's no changing them. Some resolutions have force—they require action by dioceses, parishes, impose penalties on clergy that violate them. These resolutions affect what's going on in churches; they say what saints we commemorate and how, who can get married and who can refuse to marry them, how much money there is to fund new churches, et cetera, et cetera, and so forth.

Other resolutions are sort of semi-doctrinal. They're positional, on topics ranging from abortion to the death penalty to gun control to Guantanamo Bay. We don't publish a catechism (beyond the short one in the Book of Common Prayer) that includes all our official doctrine. We don't write Lutheran-style "Confessions" talking through all our official beliefs. If you want to know what we believe, look at how we pray. If you want to know how we officially position ourselves, read the Episcopal Archives[3] of all the resolutions passed by General Convention. These resolutions don't need anybody to do anything; they just state our position on an issue like gun control, immigration, or police brutality. Lots of folks have argued that we don't need these resolutions, that we should get rid of them entirely, make the convention shorter, less argumentative. But, like most humans, we all want to get rid of the ones we don't like, and keep the ones we do like, so we can never agree on which resolutions to 86.

Non-Stop[4]

Deputies and bishops are kept pretty busy during convention. There are ten legislative days and a LOT of material to get through. But like any good con, General Convention includes time for worship and play. There are panels, workshops, hymn sings, receptions, an exhibition hall, book signings, selfies with celebs, prayer meetings, parties, and good times.

There are too many for any one individual to attend—so pick your poison. Would you rather wine and dine with the bishop of Virginia[5] or pray with the members of the Acts 8 Movement? Would you rather attend the Integrity Eucharist[6] or go to your seminary dinner?[7] While our work is holy, we believe that fellowship and play are holy too, and General Convention is a great time for people who haven't seen one another in decades to catch up, to meet people in person you've only interacted with online, and to enjoy the diversity present in the Episcopal Church.

A group of Episcopalians who believe the church has reached an "**Acts 8 Moment**," where God is calling us to preach resurrection and not death, made its debut at the 2012 General Convention. These guys are planting new churches, trying creative online ministry, and generally revitalizing the church.[8]

The most popular event, obviously, is the daily Eucharist held at the mid-morning break. Each day we gather to praise God together, and to celebrate the many gifts present in our church. The liturgy style varies from traditional to jazzy, incorporating music from the Black Church tradition, from different Native congregations, to drums and gongs from a Korean congregation. Bishops from all over the church preside, and the organizers choose the best guest preachers around. You've never sung hymns like you've sung with five thousand other Episcopalians, all of whom are belting their lungs out. And there's something special about sharing in communion with so many other souls committed to the glory of God.

But there's more worship available than just the official stuff. Organizations such as the previously mentioned Integrity, the Union of Black Episcopalians, and more hold prayer meetings and Eucharists. And of course deputations, communities of vowed religious, or individuals in their hotel rooms can pray the Daily Office.

Once you've offered your prayers, it's time for the receptions. There are literally hundreds of these; I can't possibly describe them all. Just know that if you're young, scrappy, and hungry, there's no night of the week that you'll starve.

Take a Break

Even if you're a deputy or a bishop, there will be times when you can get a break during the day—so make sure you check out the exhibit hall. This enormous room is filled with a breathtaking variety of exhibitors, all of whom totally want you to stop at their table, and are willing to give you pins and buttons for the favor of your attention.

> Some call DFMS the "national" church. But the Episcopal Church spans many more countries than just the United States. Sometimes you'll hear it refered to as "815"—which refers to the address of its headquarters at 815 Second Avenue in New York City—as shorthand. The Episcopal Church is an international body, with dioceses and congregations located throughout the world.

The biggest booth is always that of the Domestic and Foreign Missionary Society, sometimes in concert with the United Thank Offering. DFMS is the official and legal name of the Episcopal Church; that is, the church-wide office of the whole denomination. DFMS sets up an enormous display, featuring the good work being done by the United Thank Offering, Episcopal Relief and Development, and others.

> **The United Thank Offering**, or UTO, was set up by the Women's Auxiliary to the Board of Missions of the Domestic and Foreign Missionary Society in the late 1800s to fund the mission of the church. The UTO In-gathering (collected donations from local congregations through their diocese) at the 78th General Convention in 2015 totaled over $4 million.[9]

Episcopal Relief & Development: Sometimes called ER-D for short, this is the primary development and relief organization of the Episcopal Church, providing resources in emergency situations around the world.[10]

The seminaries of the Episcopal Church each have a booth, as do many dioceses, religious orders, booksellers, and vestment-makers. The exhibit hall offers you the chance to dress up like a bishop, buy wood carvings from Jerusalem, talk with eager seminarians about why their theological training is *the* absolute bestest in all the land, get books signed by your favorite authors (hint, hint), and more.

The World Is Wide Enough

The Episcopal Church, as aforementioned, was originally an outpost of the Church of England in the shiny new colonies of the Americas. The Church of England went with its colonists all over the world, mixing somewhat the Good News of Jesus Christ with the ofttimes bad news of British rule. The first church to separate from the mother was the Scottish Episcopal Church (*not* the Church of Scotland—that's Presbyterian), which went its own way without acrimony or bloodshed in 1689.

The year 1689 was also the time of the **Glorious Revolution**, when William and Mary kicked the Scottish Catholic Stuarts off the throne. That did involve *some* bloodshed (though rather less than expected), but while intimately connected with the religion of the monarch, not so much with the Scottish Episcopal Church, ken? (Forgive my attempt at Scottish brogue. It willnae happen again.)

Aside from that intra-island difference, all other provinces of the Anglican tradition were intimately connected with, and owed their loyalty to, the Church of England throughout the colonial era. When those pesky Americans decided to continue in the Anglican way of being Christian but not stay part of the Church of England, they inadvertently created what is now known as the Anglican Communion.

From the beginning, the communion has never really known what it was. A collection of churches who share a common heritage, a common history, though somewhat at war with that painful history. A global community based on common prayer, even though we all have different prayer books. Christians who view staying in communion with the See (Archbishop) of Canterbury as crucial, even if they can't stand being in communion with one another at times.

Let's break it down:

The Anglican Communion is comprised of thirty-eight autonomous provinces in 127 countries all over the world. There are over 85 million Anglicans, mostly on the continent of Africa, but also in South America, New Zealand, India, France, Canada, Haiti, and more. Each province is governed in its own way, by its own canons, but voluntarily holds itself accountable to the others for the sake of relationship. Basically, we try to all live together in harmony, but everything changes if the Fire Nation attacks.

In the twentieth century, when we decided to get more formal about this sort of thing, we set up Four Instruments of Unity. None of these instruments, separately or together, have the authority to make decisions or issue edicts, but we have agreed that they are important. It is Christ's love that binds us together, but these instruments make manifest that binding, outward and visible signs of an inward and already-present truth. The instruments are:

The Archbishop of Canterbury

Ever since the very impressively British-sounding Synod of Whitby 1,400 years ago, Christians following the Anglican way have acknowledged the primacy of the See of Canterbury. The archbishop isn't the same as the pope. He (or, theoretically, she, but it's always been a he so far) does not rule by fiat. He presides at the table. He's basically the DM. He doesn't write the rules, but he presides over the adventure and guides the players.

The Anglican Consultative Council

This is an extremely recent invention—a community of laity, clergy, and bishops that meets every two to three years to debate and discuss all kinds of matters relevant to the communion. Their goal is to serve the member churches and enable networks of ministry. Aka ACC.

The Primates' Meeting

Each province is headed by a presiding bishop, an archbishop, or a primus, and all these folks collectively are called primates. (No, they're not monkeys. That joke is getting old.) They have no formal authority as a body, but value one another's support and friendship as they serve as the servant to the servants of God in their provinces.

Lambeth Conference

This gathering (every ten years or so) of every single bishop in the Anglican Communion has existed since 1867, much longer than the ACC or the Primates' Meeting. Lambeth Conference isn't intended to be a governing meeting, though it does pass resolutions that it intends to see followed through. It makes for a great photo op with all those purple cassocks.

The problem is that as the communion has begun to formalize its structures, and give its conversations meaning, it's beginning to punch above its weight; that is, to act as though the small amount of power it has is really a great deal of power. Thirty-eight autonomous provinces agree to submit to the instruments of unity for the sake of communion, to continue walking with one another, but they remain autonomous. The communion has no power to force any of these independent bodies to do its will; they choose to, or not, out of their love for Christ and one another.

Which, in the last fifteen years or so, has led to a fair amount of conflict. The state of this not-nation (and the federation of not-states) has been troubled since the 1990s (if not longer) over issues relating to human sexuality, marriage, and the decline of Western power. The exact cause and nature of the conflict depends on one's perspective, but consider this: The Church has always, from its earliest days, practiced what we call *marginal differentiation*. Marginal differentiation encourages groups of people who are basically similar to exaggerate the differences between them. Think of Trekkies versus *Star Wars* fans—they have so much in common, and yet, they exaggerate the differences. (One is a space opera and the other a never-ending adventure. One values teamwork and togetherness and the other focuses on good versus evil.) You see this in small churches in rural Texas, too, when the Presbyterians, Methodists, and Episcopalians all offer the exact same Vacation Bible School program, but all describe it very differently. We've always done this—you see this in Scripture as the early Christians exaggerate the differences between them and their Jewish brothers and sisters.

And Anglicans are doing this too, as we speak. What draws us together is much greater than that which pulls us apart: the love of Jesus, who incorporates us into the mystical body of Christ; a common heritage of common prayer valued beyond common belief; an emphasis on sacramental experience as closer to God than listening to the Word. There are networks of relationships across the communion: between Canadian Anglicans and Ugandan Anglicans, between Ghanaian Anglicans and American Episcopalians, between New Zealanders and Indians, South Africans and Germans, you get the idea. But we spit on these relationships and destroy the ties that bind for the sake of playing up differences between us to maneuver through local politics.

The world is wide enough for all of us. That is the essential truth of the Anglican Communion. And if we behave like Aaron Burr, too young and blind to see that, then the communion will fracture. So wonks, we've got to get our acts together. We've got to marshal our forces against marginal differentiation, and focus on that which binds us together. Discord is our enemy, and any enemy of our enemy is a friend. Stand firm in your training, and remember to always use your powers for good.

Magic
The God Part

In which we peer behind the veil to see what's really going on

The title of this chapter is enough to disconcert a lot of Christians. Many Christians are not comfortable thinking about theology, or anything that we do, as magic.

So what is magic? How is it different from theology? Jonathan Strange says that magicians and priests sow in the same field but magicians sow wheat and priests sow rye—meaning that magicians and clergymen will never agree.[1] But is that true? The main difference between magic and religion is *reliability* and *who has the power*.

Depending on the universe, magic works the same way every time. If you say the incantation properly, it will work, no matter what. In *The Magicians*, Lev Grossman imagines a world in which magical incantation differs depending on the circumstances but still: Magic relies on the caster.[2] On his skill, on his knowledge, on his power.

Theology, on the other hand, relies on the Caster. On God, the maker of all things. Human beings, no matter their order, have no power in ourselves to help ourselves. It is God's power. God often chooses human beings to work through, but the power is not their own. Plus, God, while trustworthy, does not always move in a predictable way. As C. S. Lewis writes about Aslan, his stand-in for Jesus in *The Chronicles of Narnia* series, "Who said anything about safe? 'Course he isn't safe. But he's good. He's the King, I tell you."[3] Jesus said it this way, "For [God] makes the sun rise on the evil and on the good, and sends rain on the righteous and on the unrighteous."[4] And yet, God is not just some great cosmic dice, coming up with a 1 sometimes and a 20 others. God has loaded the dice in our favor, God has completed the quest already but allows us to find our own way through the Adventure Path, and God invites us into relationship that includes the evil and the unrighteous, with all the messiness that entails. The Paladin shall lie down with the Anti-Paladin, and the dwarf and the giant shall eat together. They shall not hurt or destroy on all God's holy mountain.

> Almighty God, you know that we have no power in ourselves to help ourselves: Keep us both outwardly in our bodies and inwardly in our souls, that we may be defended from all adversities which may happen to the body, and from all evil thoughts which may assault and hurt the soul. Amen.[5]

In the meantime, what theology does the average geek need to know, when beginning this quest we call the Christian life? What background content do we need to download before getting started? How does this affect us now?

Baptism

Baptism is our entry point. It's how we get initiated, it's the way in, it's the Wardrobe that leads us into another world—or really, a radically new way of experiencing our world. There's a comic I've seen floating around the web that claims baptism gives a person a +1 to their save against the devil. That's pretty funny, and it's a popular conception, but it's not actually how baptism works. Baptism is more than a nice bath (or, more likely, a sprinkle, at least in most Episcopal churches). Baptism is more than a shield charm against the spiritual forces of evil. Baptism is death. Baptism is resurrection to new life. Here's what the Bible says:

> Do you not know that all of us who have been baptized into Christ Jesus were baptized into his death? Therefore we have been buried with him by baptism into death, so that, just as Christ was raised from the dead by the glory of the Father, so we too might walk in newness of life. For if we have been united with him in a death like his, we will certainly be united with him in a resurrection like his. We know that our old self was crucified with him so that the body of sin might be destroyed, and we might no longer be enslaved to sin. For whoever has died is freed from sin. But if we have died with Christ, we believe that we will also live with him.[6]

It also says:

> For this perishable body must put on imperishability, and this mortal body must put on immortality. When this perishable body puts on imperishability, and this mortal body puts on immortality, then the saying that is written will be fulfilled: Death has been swallowed up in victory.[7]

In baptism, we die. Not as dramatically as the followers of the Drowned God in *A Song of Ice and Fire*—nobody's thumping your chest to bring you back to life after literally drowning—but we die. We die to sin, which the apostle Paul personifies as one of the principalities and powers that enslaves us—body and soul. We die to self, to the part of us that does the things we do not want, and the part that does things that hurt other people. We die to our individuality, because when we rise again, we have been incorporated into the Body of Christ, as constituent members of Christ himself, the Church.

> For in the one Spirit we were all baptized into one body— Jews or Greeks, slaves or free—and we were all made to drink of one Spirit.[8]

This doesn't mean that after we're baptized we're perfect. Not that anyone thought that—through the Crusades, early twentieth-century lynch mobs, child sex abusers, colonial violence, and so much more, Christians have been offering proof of our continued sinfulness even after dying to sin and rising with Christ. So what gives? How does sin maintain such a hold on us, even after so dramatic and life-altering an initiation as death itself?

And if baptism is death, how is it also a promise? Episcopalians love to talk about the Baptismal Covenant (which, even though we believe anyone baptized in the name of the Father, the Son, and the Holy Spirit is really for real baptized, is unique to us) as our founding charge and promise. It is a covenant between us and God, we say, wherein we make promises to God and God makes promises to us in return. Like a marriage. We have responsibilities to God, and to God's other children on behalf of God, that we voluntarily make. That's not very deathlike at all. Death just happens to us, we just fall through the veil without thinking, without planning, without expecting it. We don't make any promises, and we're not wearing special white, lacy gowns. [Return to "The Ultimate Quest," page 14, for a review if needed.]

Baptism is both a death and a covenant, something that happens with our consent and beyond the bounds of our understanding. It is both. You'll see this throughout this chapter. Christian theology often—and Episcopal theology even more so—relies on paradox. We embrace the tension of *both/and* rather than *either/*

or. This can be tricky for those of us whose natural state is to view things in black and white, those who have trouble with contradictory things being true at the same time. I'm afraid I'm going to have to ask you to accept that as a game mechanic in this 'verse.[9] Baptism is only the first paradoxical, oxymoronic of our topics because now we move on to . . .

Sin

Sin is a dirty word in modern American conversation. In the last two hundred years or so, Christians have too often reduced sin solely to wrong sex at the wrong time and with the wrong person. While we acknowledge things like murder and theft as sinful too, let's not forget that, in living memory, Christians have authorized preemptive war, torture of prisoners, exclusion of refugees from war-torn countries, and the amassing of truly egregious piles of wealth as Not Sinful. This has led to some misperceptions about sin among those who would otherwise journey on the Christian pilgrimage.

But geeks—we know about Sin. It is all up in our stuff. Sin is the Fire Nation attacking, instead of living in harmony with the other nations. Sin is the Empire silencing thousands of voices just to test the deadly firepower of its new space station. Sin (upper case) is the Capitol demanding the sacrifice of children for its entertainment in punishment for ancient rebellion.

Christians talk about sin in two ways: Sin as an external concept, an existential evil (the First Evil, if you will, *Buffy* fans), a power and principality that gains control over us—possesses us in a very real way, a sickness that infects us. Sin (lower case) is also an action, something that we do, that we choose to do, that harms other beings whom God loves and breaches our relationship with them. Christ's death on the cross and resurrection defeated this first kind of Sin, the First Evil sin, the great beast that wraps itself around us like a python coming to choke the life out of us, the power that enslaves us and makes us incapable of seeing beyond our own selfish desires. But obviously, little-s sins continue to happen. We see them every time a police officer uses excessive force, every time a stockbroker embezzles money from his employer or unduly risks her client's savings, every time a spouse raises a hand in violence against their partner. We see them as we envy the newest iPhone we can't afford to upgrade yet, as we cut off another driver in our hurry, as we're short with the girl at the cash register for something that's not her fault.

"I must not fear. **Fear is the mind-killer.** Fear is the little-death that brings total obliteration. I will face my fear. I will permit it to pass over me and through me. And when it has gone past I will turn the inner eye to see its path. Where the fear has gone there will be nothing. Only I will remain."[10]

Sin is the enemy. It is the mind-killer (and yes, fear is definitely essential to sin). It is our life's work to defeat it, but we are incapable of defeating it. This is only one of the paradoxes of Christian living. No one yet born of woman, save the One, has gone without sin. But to lie down in defeat, to give up and declare that we might as well enjoy being evil, is impossible to imagine. I cannot stress this enough: Our sin hurts other people. It is not a victimless crime—even coveting, which seems like something we could easily do without anyone knowing, changes our hearts and coats them with greed. We begin to rationalize our actions in the face of this new desire for more.

Neurologists say that cheating on tests or plagiarism don't start out as big crimes, they start small. We get lazy with our references or we tell ourselves that our eyes just happened to wander over to that paper. Then, over time, we begin to move the line just enough that we can justify truly blatant stealing of others' intellectual property.[11] It's the same with other sins. Jesus tells us that he who calls his brother a fool has murdered him in his heart,[12] and the more we call others names, the more we dehumanize them as somehow "Other," the more likely we are to feel justified in harming them.

So what is to be done about sin? First, Sin must be our enemy. It is that which we set our face against. We who have died to Sin in baptism must combat it with every fiber of our being. We must root it out, like citizens of Pern rooting out the green that attracts the Thread. Second, we must direct our combat against ourselves. We have met the enemy, and he is us. Jesus tells us that we cannot take the speck out of our brother's eye without first removing the log from our own.[13] He also said that those without sin should be the first to condemn others[14]—and none of us is without sin.[15]

Finally, we must have the humility to admit that over Sin we cannot be victorious. Even though Christ has freed us from bondage to sin and death, it continues. In God's infinite wisdom, we are left to continue the struggle against this enemy. Already but not yet has it been defeated. And this paradox will be true until Christ comes again. And so our humility must drive us to yet more mercy for those who are also greatly afflicted by the Sin-beast as we are. For that is its true defeat; not that we should be purified and clean, but that we might strip it of its power to define our worth. For God's power is made perfect in weakness.[16]

Sin's greatest enemy is confession. Scripture says, "If we confess our sins, he who is faithful and just will forgive us our sins and cleanse us from all unrighteousness."[17] Candor is the answer. By being honest about our shortcomings, we continually humble ourselves. Confession reminds us to be merciful to others, who are sinners just as we are. And in our mercy, we imitate him whose mercy sets us free from sin.

God

El. YHWH. The King of the Universe. Adonai. Creator. Father. Almighty. Christians call our deity by many names, but there is only one God. Yes, it's true, the Bible hints at the possibility that there might be other gods, just worse ones than the God of Abraham, Isaac, and Jacob, but at least by the time of Elijah (which is about three thousand years ago), it's pretty clear that those who worshipped the God that Christians now claim as our own had successfully proved to their satisfaction that their God was it.

No one has ever seen God, and we don't know what God looks like. The old guy with a white beard that we meet in *Monty Python and the Holy Grail* is as likely a candidate as Alanis Morisette in *Dogma*. We believe that human beings, both male and female, are made in the image of God,[18] but it's never made clear in the Bible that image means appearance. The New Testament also tells us that Jesus Christ is the image of the invisible God.[19] Again, this may or may not be in appearance. But it's not wrong, or primitive, or simplistic for us to attribute human-like characteristics to God.

Episcopalians have long been famous for what's called the "three-legged stool" of **Scripture**, **tradition**, and **reason** to help us form our theology, to help us form the way that we look at God. My theology professor taught us, though, that it's less a stool with three equal parts, and more like a telescope. We're looking through the scope at God, and the farthest lens from us, the one closest to God, is Scripture. Scripture reveals to us God's character, how God has behaved in history, and most especially what God has revealed of God's self in the person of Jesus Christ.

But we look at Scripture through the lens of tradition. We are not capable of looking at Scripture without all the baggage of the way we have historically looked at Scripture. Even the way we translate the words into English is based on how we have translated those words before. In some ways, this is good. C. S. Lewis encourages us to read old books because, while our predecessors certainly made mistakes, they made different ones than we are liable to make because of their different customs and culture. Tradition grounds us in a living path of those who also knew God, so that we make sure we are walking in the way of our forebears.

"So if it seems to you that you have understood the divine scriptures, or any part of them, in such a way that by this understanding you do not build up this twin love of God and neighbor, then you have not yet understood them." Augustine, *De Doctrina Christiana*, written in 397, so you know he's no liberal, free-love hippie.

We also look at the lens of tradition through the lens of reason. We use our brains, our experience, and our culture today to help us interpret where the tradition might have led us astray. Augustine of Hippo, writing for his time (around 1,600 years ago), urged his readers that if they interpreted Scripture in such a way that did not lead them to greater love of God and of neighbor, then they had not read them correctly. In other words, they were not using the lenses of reason and tradition at the right focus to be able to see the God that Scripture was trying to show them.

So what is the character of God as shown to us in the Scriptures? God is shown to be creative, generative, fruitful, righteous, faithful, with a strong love for particular individuals and for the human race as a whole. God liberates, God guides, God dispenses Law—and that Law shows us further elements of God's character. Christians, often, misguidedly dismiss the Law as something outdated, undone by the saving act of Christ, or both. At best, this is supercessionist; at worst, it's openly anti-Semitic. God gave us the Law not to punish us, but to protect us from one another.

Even the apostle Paul, noted Law-hater, wrote to the Galatians that the Law was our guardian, showing us the way in our youth. The Law includes dietary restrictions and purity rituals that we no longer observe, yes, but it also commands the people of Israel to leave large portions of their crop for the poor, and to care for the orphan and widow. It proclaims that strangers and aliens should be treated the same as the native-born. It ensures that elderly mothers and fathers are not forgotten when they are too old to work. At its heart, the Law is about protecting us from the sins that other people would commit against us. And while that cannot save us from death and Jesus can, it retains value in that protection.

Scripture also tells us that the heavens declare the glory of God,[20] so we are justified in looking to the natural world as evidence for God's character. This area of study is called *natural theology* and has been practiced since at least the time of Thomas Aquinas. This idea is not some New Age-y, twentieth-century treehugger invention. The character of God as shown to us in nature is one that finds beauty in a truly dizzying array of diversity. There are literally millions of species that God created. If we look beyond earth to stars in their multitude,[21] it is staggering to think of God's handiwork, the work of his fingers.[22]

Scripture and the natural world teach us about the character of God. But Christians believe that the truest view we can see of God comes in the person of Jesus Christ. Early-twentieth-century theologian Karl Barth writes that our faith is not in some vague, unseen presence that controls the world. We have a name for who God is, what God looks like. That name is:

Jesus

Christians are most closely identified with the person of Jesus. "Christian," after all, is derived from the Greek word for Christ-follower. It's no wonder that Jesus looms large over the other Persons of the Trinity, being the only one that human beings have actually met in the flesh.

As we've already discussed, Jesus is the image of the invisible God. The Bible calls him "Emmanu-El," God with us. God, the Creator and Ruler of the Universe, believes that we are important enough to sacrifice the phenomenal, cosmic power and enter an itty-bitty living space to be with us, not as a Genie but as one of us.[23] Not only did Jesus Christ, the Word of God, dwell among us, God also became flesh. I mean that literally—Jesus was not in disguise, nor was he "veiled in flesh" as the old Christmas carol goes. He was not a new-model Cylon hiding out until "All Along the Watchtower" starts playing. Jesus literally became human, formed in the womb of Mary his mother, who was entirely human, and retained his divinity at the same time without mixing the two. In so doing, he made human flesh capable of bearing the weight of divinity. Because the Word became flesh and dwelt among us, we are capable of bearing God's presence inside our own bodies.

Christians, being named after Jesus, obviously center him in our theology. But we emphasize different parts of his life and

Timey-Wimey Stuff:[24] It should be noted that this is without reference to time. While Christ's Incarnation was necessarily time-limited as he entered our reality, his saving actions are not limited to those who chronologically lived during or after that time. When John the Baptist says, "Here is the Lamb of God who takes away the sin of the world,"[25] he really means, "of the world," not "of those who have heard of Jesus and follow him." All this has happened before and all this will happen again; God is outside time, after all.

mission, depending on our own personal bent. Lutherans and Evangelicals often focus on Christ's sacrifice on the cross, our total dependence on his mercy and grace, and gratitude for his saving death. Eastern Orthodoxy features his resurrection more prominently, focusing on Christ's victory over sin and death by dying and rising again. Roman Catholics strive to follow Jesus's teachings to feed the hungry, clothe the naked, and welcome the stranger. Episcopalians remember the Incarnation, Christ emptying himself of divine power to come among us as one of us, Emmanu-El, God-with-us.

It's important to remember that all of this is a package deal. There is no Resurrection without the Crucifixion. There is no Crucifixion without Christ's subversive teachings that offend those in power. There is none of this at all without his Incarnation from the womb of Mary his mother. So while you may see different emphases depending on who you are reading, remember that all Christians believe that it's all necessary, and we can't get rid of any one point and maintain the others.

Jesus was a person. He lived a full and complete life like us in every way, except that he did not sin. He grew up as the son of Joseph, a carpenter in Nazareth, a small suburb of Sepphoris, a much larger Roman town where it's likely that he and Joseph worked. His family was devout; he was presented in the Temple in Jerusalem as their first-born, and they went to observe Passover at the Temple at least once, when he was twelve years old.[26]

As an adult, he received the baptism of John, though he had no sins for which to repent, and his Sonship of God was announced to all present by the Holy Spirit descending in the form of a dove. He healed people. He cast out demons. He performed miracles—notably feeding five thousand men plus women and children with only five loaves of bread and two fish.[27]

John's baptism, which was obviously not in the name of the Three-Personed God, is a pre-cursor to our practice of baptism but not the same. Its purpose was not to incorporate individuals into the Body of Christ, but to wash away sins from them. Jesus, in participating in this rite as the Sinless One, hallowed it and transformed it into the essential sacrament it is today.

And as he traipsed through Galilee like some kind of great, nomadic Gandalf, he also dispensed the wisdom of his teachings. We have four whole books of those teachings. There's quite a lot of overlap, of course, but each of those gospels presents a unique and different perspective on what the Lord requires of us, and contains within it stories and parables that appear nowhere else. Jesus taught of justice and mercy, and what it really means to follow the Law. He declared what liberation theologians call a "preferential option for the poor."

Preferential option for the poor: I have no idea who said this exact phrase first, but the idea comes from Latin American liberation theology, which began to be practiced in the 1960s. Pope John Paul II officially proclaimed it in his 1991 encyclical "*Centesimus annus*," so you know it's legit.

These teachings, indicting people with power and wealth, lifting up the poor, outcast, and disempowered, threatened those who had the authority to sentence him to death. He was crucified by a state that routinely practiced this method of execution. On the Third Day, he rose again. He presented himself first to the women who had come to anoint his body with spices, then to his disciples. He was able to appear in rooms wherein the door had been locked, but also was embodied, physical, capable of being touched, still bearing the scars of his crucifixion.

Three Days, Really? The math on this has never really worked. How could Jesus have died on Friday and risen on Sunday and Christians say he was in the tomb three days? It's important to remember that Jewish days begin at sundown the night before. He dies on Friday (which began Thursday night); that is the first day. He remains in the tomb as his disciples observe the Sabbath that begins Friday night and stays through Saturday. That's the second day. He rises again on Sunday, which begins at sundown (and is often celebrated by Episcopalians on) Saturday, the third day.

In recent years, Christians in the West have tended to say that the most important part of following this Jesus was for an individual Christian to have an individual relationship with Jesus; this idea was rather effectively mocked by "Buddy Christ" in *Dogma* in the '90s. It's one of those things that is *sorta* true: Jesus spent his life on earth caring for and loving individuals. He built relationships with women and men who were too often nameless, faceless parts of a crowd for whom those in power did not care. Peter. Mary Magdalene. Levi, later called Matthew. The widow who gave all she had to the Temple. The Samaritan woman at the village well. Jesus also calls us to care for these individuals as though each were he. But Scripture also teaches us that Jesus loves us as a community. In baptism, we are incorporated into "the mystical body of [God's] Son."[28] We are one body and individually members of it. So an individual's personal relationship with Jesus matters much less than what Jesus has done for us all. It's a perk, not essential.

Paul actually says, in writing the bulk of the letters in the New Testament, that there is no such thing as individual salvation, no such thing as a personal relationship with Jesus. Paul's theology relies on a Christian's incorporation, through baptism, into the Body of Christ. This incorporation is indissoluble. It is individual only in the sense that your baptism is your unique entry point into this relationship. But once the baptizee is in, the relationship with Jesus is a communal one. The Church, the Bride of Christ, is mystically in union with Christ, the Bridegroom. Individuals are only part of the Church. So let's take a look more closely at . . .

Salvation

Christians talk about salvation a lot (probably too much, honestly; there's a lot more to being a Christian than obsessing over who's saved—answer: everybody), but what does it mean? What are we being saved from? How does it work?

While there's some debate on both points, the simple answer is this: We are saved, we are liberated from being under the oppressive authority of Sin and Death. And we are saved through the life, death, and resurrection of Jesus Christ. Let's take it point by point:

The Garden of Eden

While the Garden of Eden is a metaphor, not a documentary recording of actual events, it captures our relationship with God thusly: All nations and races, created of God, loving God, lived together in harmony. Everything changed when the Serpent Nation attacked. Only God, acting in and among and through humankind, could stop it.

While it's silly to make an exact parallel with *Avatar: The Last Airbender,* the two stories are not unalike. Sin and the power of Death crept in to our world and took hold of us. We were powerless over them, and we continued to pursue our selfish goals, to seek power over others, to abuse and hurt any who were unable to defend themselves. And we died. But God, who made Creation and called it good, would not have it so.

The Law

God sent the Law and the prophets to show us the right way to live. But the Sin-beast still had us under his thumb. We knew the right way to live—loving our neighbor, caring for orphan and widow—but we did not. We still wanted power, riches, glory, and our own way. We sought to remake every nation in our image, united under one Fire Lord, and we disdained the diversity that God built into God's masterwork. Those who followed the Law, like Jet, became impatient for the victory to be assured, and wound up perpetrating crimes as bad as those of the enemy. By placing the authority of the Law and the purity of God above the welfare of human beings, these Law-obsessed people abused and hurt those less capable than they of maintaining perfection and surviving.

Love

Behold the Lamb of God, then, who came to show us not only victory, but a new way to victory. Consider: The disciples spent much of Jesus's ministry telling him he must focus his energy on driving the oppressive Roman force away from Judea, just as Sokka, Katara, Suki, Toph, and Zuko focus their energy on helping Aang to kill the Fire Lord. But Aang, like Jesus, finds another way, a spirit-bending way, an ancient way to re-order the world according to God's first principles. Jesus, too, refuses to endorse a revolution that takes the lives of others and names another race of people as the enemy. Instead, he becomes the recipient of violence, taking upon himself the iniquity of us all, and responds with love, rather than violence.

That love is the Deep Magic C. S. Lewis describes in *The Lion, the Witch, and the Wardrobe*, the love that empowers the reversal of Death itself.[29] By refusing to participate in our warfare, refusing to seek power and glory for himself, refusing to privilege his own concerns over the needs of humanity, Jesus surprised the powers of Sin and Death just as assuredly as Harry Potter surprised Voldemort. "This cold-blooded walk to his own destruction would require a different kind of bravery."[30] This bespeaks a different kind of victory than that to which we have become accustomed.

Salvation

This victory not only saves us, but it also turns the world upside down, declaring that all we have thought and believed and practiced about power and success and righteousness has been wrong. James Cone and Reinhold Niebuhr write that the cross transvalues human values;[31] that is, it changes our whole way of looking at the world. Rather than admiring those with money and power, we are called to live as people who value great love and nonviolence, who return not evil with evil, but overcome evil with good.[32]

As you may recall, Thomas Cranmer was the archbishop of Canterbury from 1533 to 1556, wrote the very first Book of Common Prayer, and presided over our transition from being the (Roman Catholic) Church in England to becoming the Church of England. Cranmer settled these questions of salvation by separating them into three constituent parts, all of which work together. [Return to "The Player's Handbook," page 22, for a Cranmer refresher.]

First: We were justified, made right with God, presented as righteous and clean and perfect through the merits of Jesus Christ on the cross in Roman-occupied Jerusalem, sometime in the late 20s CE. This event is in the past perfect. It is complete. Nothing can change it.

We are now, individually and collectively, on our journey wherein we are being sanctified, made holy, made sacred, made godly, through our cooperation with the Holy Spirit. This is present tense continuous. It is in progress. The Holy Spirit is the primary actor, but this is the only step of the process in which we have an active role. This is the only place that involves us; the only part that we can affect at all.

And yet, whether we participate fully or sit back and wait for the Holy Spirit, we trust that, on the Last Day, when Christ shall come again to be our Judge, we shall be saved, fully, from the power of Sin and Death. When someone asks if you've been saved, the answer, for an Episcoplian, "Not yet, but I trust the promise of Jesus that I will be at the Last Day." This is future event. It hasn't happened yet. But we are promised that it will.

Let's take a minute at look at the second part of that process, the sanctification part, as we explore . . .

The Holy Spirit

The Holy Spirit is the trickiest of the persons of the Holy Trinity. Only alluded to in Scripture, and never as totally independent of the Father and the Son, she plays the rather thankless role of supporting and sanctifying the Church in an incorporeal and unseen way, all too often used as a pawn by those who would claim her sanction on whatever they would prefer to do.

Why refer to the Holy Spirit as a she? The Greek word *pneuma*, from which we get Spirit, is neutral—neither masculine nor feminine—which fits this never-fully-incarnately-physical being. But the English pronoun "it" is dehumanizing, and the singular "they" is not quite precise enough for tough Trinitarian theological work. Since we know that Jesus was Incarnated as a man, and referred to God as his Father, a masculine term, many Christians speak of the Holy Spirit as she to recognize the presence of the feminine amidst the Divine.

The Spirit is mentioned, Christians believe (though our Jewish friends would dispute) in the very first chapter in the Bible, as God begins the creation of the universe. She broods over the water in Creation as the breath of God (the Hebrew words for "breath" and "spirit" being the same—*ruach*). Shortly before the time of Jesus, there came about a Jewish tradition that personified Wisdom into an almost god-like being. This tradition claimed that Wisdom was the first thing that God created, and through her (look at the book of Proverbs to learn more about Lady Wisdom), all other things were created. Some scholars say that she acted basically as God's wife for this segment of the Jewish community.

Other scholars would say that the **Lady Wisdom** mentioned in ancient Jewish Wisdom literature more closely matches Jesus Christ, the Word of God. Philo of Alexandria, a Jewish scholar in Egypt who lived shortly before the coming of Jesus, felt uncomfortable with a feminine consort for God, so he began to refer to Wisdom (*sophia* in Greek) as instead Word (*logos* in Greek). Suffice it to say, there's some imprecision of terminology here.

The Holy Spirit is breath, the Holy Spirit is wisdom, the Holy Spirit is a lot of things unseen; that is, until the day of Jesus's baptism by John in the river Jordan. The gospels assert that the Holy Spirit descended upon Jesus in the form of a dove, the symbol of peace. But throughout the rest of Jesus's ministry she stays hidden, though Jesus keeps promising his disciples that he will send her as Comforter, as Advocate after he has gone. I don't know about you, but I don't find tongues of flame terribly comforting, though that is how she showed herself at Pentecost. The disciples heard a rushing wind, and then suddenly, tongues of flame alit upon their heads and gave them supernatural, charismatic abilities, including the ability to speak in other languages to the people gathered.[33]

The Holy Spirit seems to have returned to a largely unseen role in our modern age. While there are denominations that believe they receive spiritual gifts—even that receiving gifts is necessary for all baptized people—and most Christians believe the Holy Spirit plays a role comforting, guiding, encouraging, and challenging God's people, most of us have never seen her, in the form of a dove or anything else. She's the Force without a dark side, that which empowers all that we do, but never seen. A priest I worked with said that she acts not unlike radio waves, or air: She acts invisibly, but her invisibility does not mean she's not present.

The Holy Spirit is perhaps the most controversial of the Three Persons of the Trinity. She appears only briefly in Scripture, brooding over the waters in Genesis, descending on Jesus at his baptism, and again in the form of tongues of fire on the disciples at Pentecost. She never speaks for herself. We never learn her teachings; she gives no commandments. Her enigmatic interactions with humankind lend themselves to constant reinterpretation, some kind of Rorschach test for Christians (and observers of Christians) to project their opinions onto.

Her role unclear, her being even more so, the Holy Spirit is one of those truths who is stranger than fiction—the kind of character that no DM would allow, because she's so broken that no rules could possibly apply to her. The kind of character no editor would publish, because she's so indefinable no reader could relate. Two thousand years, and we still don't understand her. The Church really only acknowledges her when we talk about . . .

The Holy Trinity

Ah, the Holy Trinity: one of the most misunderstood doctrines in the Church, usually by Christians. George R.R. Martin himself misunderstood it when he modeled the Faith of the Seven[34] after it—but in his defense, the *way* he got it wrong was the way most people get it wrong: The Trinity is not one god with three faces, or identities, or modalities. Nor is the Trinity three gods— you will never hear Christians talk about "the gods" the way the Lannisters, Starks, and Tyrells do. Talking about the Trinity without straying into heresy is a tricky task, and not one that we do well. It's best to leave it a mystery so far as we can. The prayer book says:

> There is but one living and true God, everlasting, without body, parts, or passions; of infinite power, wisdom, and goodness; the Maker, and Preserver of all things both visible and invisible. And in the unity of this Godhead there be three Persons, of one substance, power, and eternity; the Father, the Son, and the Holy Ghost.[35]

Let's take these words one at a time:

One

God is the only God, and God is one.

Living

God is alive. Perhaps not in any way that we could recognize. Does God breathe, for instance? If so, what does God breathe? Oxygen? From where? But God is living, not dead.

True

There are a lot of possible meanings here. The definition could be calling any other definitions of God false—thus calling out any who don't agree with its doctrine of the Trinity. Or it could be describing God as true—loyal, steadfast, reliable. I lean toward the latter, but I can't pretend the first isn't a reasonable interpretation.

Everlasting

God is eternal, out of time. God will not end. Death is not the end. The eventual implosion of the universe is not the end. God is above, outside, and beyond all ends.

Without body, parts, or passions

God is not tangible, divisible, or hormonal. We know that God is humanlike in some ways; if we are made in God's image, then God must be like us in *some way*. But the prayer book rules out the similarities being physical. God does not have a physical body that can be depicted in imagery. All images of God that you see in statues or stained glass are therefore metaphors and should be interpreted as such. God also can't be divided (see my previous statements that there are not three gods). God is one, by definition. Finally, God does not have passions. Some of our Bible stories appear to contradict this. God definitely gets passionately angry at the Israelites on several occasions, but what this means is that God is not driven by preferences. God loves all, and is not passionate about one over another (sorry, sports fans!).

Of infinite power, wisdom, and goodness

God's power, wisdom, and goodness are without limit. The limit does not exist. They are utterly un-understandable by our puny human brains. Now, some people use this reality to ascribe to God some truly odd positions, and to defend themselves against those who disagree. After all, if God's ways go beyond our understanding, then they needn't conform to common sense. So if someone makes a common sense response to an unlikely doctrine, some will abuse this idea by saying that common sense doesn't matter, since we can't understand God's ways. God's wisdom and goodness really are infinite, and beyond our understanding. But we can only act within the limits of our understanding, and within the example God has given us through the lenses of Scripture, tradition, and reason. Think of it like a game mechanic. Sometimes, it doesn't totally make logical sense, but those are the rules we all agree to work with.

The Maker and Preserver of all things

God created everything. And, important to our discussion of the Trinity, all three Persons of the Trinity created everything. Because we think of fathers as creators, and not sons or spirits, and because the Hebrew Scriptures speak of God as One, we tend to think of creation as all the Father's work. But the Scriptures make clear that all of God participated in the creation of the universe.

In unity of this Godhead there be three Persons

George R.R. Martin's Faith of the Seven is not unlike some modern believers who want to attribute to God various roles and personalities. And seven is a powerful number in the Christian tradition, just as well as three. But over two thousand years, Christians have only ever claimed three Persons in the Godhead.

The Father, the Son, and the Holy Ghost

These are the traditional titles ascribed to the three Persons of the Trinity. Jesus speaks of God as his Father in all four gospels and throughout his ministry. Jesus being a man, and being related to God as Father, makes him the Son. The Holy Ghost (or Spirit, in modern translations) is never seen, and Jesus gives her multiple titles: Comforter, Advocate, Guide, and Spirit.

As the Church has begun to expand our thinking about God, and particularly about God's relationship with human beings, we have begun to question the wisdom of referring to God with exclusively masculine titles and exclusively masculine pronouns. This has led to some churches blessing in the name of "the Creator, the Redeemer, the Sustainer," invoking "the One, Holy, and Undivided Trinity," and concluding Psalms with "Glory be to our Mother, Redeemer, and to the Holy of Holies."[36]

There are many in the Church who are not comfortable with this move. Straying from the titles Jesus gave us is a frightening thing, which communicates a great deal about our theology. The first of these alternative formulations particularly has come in for criticism, due to its perceived modalism (that heresy that Martin replicates in *ASOIAF*). Naming God, then, remains a work in progress, as we hold disparate goals in tension.

Now that we have explored who God is, it's time for us to talk about what we are asked to do, if we embark on this quest of following God. This work is called:

Ministry

One of the biggest misconceptions that has prospered in the Church for the last 1,600 years or so is this idea that ministry is something only clerics can do. Unless you fit into a certain class (what we call order of ministry), you can't be a minister of the Word of God. This is obvious nonsense directly contradicted by a plain reading of Scripture, of the words of Jesus himself. "Whoever is not against us is for us."[37] Ministry is not something professionally educated, collar-wearing types do. It is not something done within the cloisters of the church. Ministry is the

Christian life. It is what we are about. All baptized Christians are in the party.

Each order of ministry is called to do something different. [Go to "Classes" on page 45 for a refresher.] But what does our theology say about human activity? If all life is meant to be in the service of Christ, what ethics are we called to?

When Jesus was asked to summarize the Law, he boiled it down to the Great Commandment: You shall love the Lord your God with all your heart, with all your soul, with all your mind, and with all your strength, and you shall love your neighbor as yourself.[38] Sometimes, Christians have treated this as two commandments— love God and love your neighbor. But what if Jesus was expounding on the commandment to love God when he tells us to love our neighbor? The way to love God is to love our neighbor as ourselves.

Professor Nichole Flores, a Roman Catholic Latina feminist moral theologian, says the answer to ethical questions is always human dignity.[39] Christians debate where Christian ethics should be rooted. Roman Catholics tend to root their ideas in the *Imago Dei*, the fact that all humans are made in the image of God and therefore should be treated as though they were God. Evangelicals tend to focus on the crucifixion of Christ, and the guilt of humankind expiated by Christ's sacrifice. Episcopalians are more likely to stick with Christ's Incarnation as the center of all our ethics. God became human in the person of Jesus Christ, thereby hallowing all human flesh with the presence of divinity. Not just the person of Jesus himself, but all human flesh. So we, Christians, are required to treat all people with respect, because the Divine is present.

All that we do is rooted in this ethic, that all human beings have sacred worth, and that we must act toward them with the same measure of love that we offer to God. Ministry, therefore, is to serve others according to the love ethic we bear toward them. And as we love them, we are proclaiming the Good News of Jesus Christ's love to them.

And at the heart of our ministry, that which always calls us back to our source, that which sustains us, nourishes us, empowers us, and challenges us to continue on this path of sanctification is . . .

Eucharist

The one thing that Jesus commanded us to do "in remembrance of me" was not to build enormous, beautiful buildings. It wasn't to read a book. It certainly wasn't to listen to some dude with a master's degree (or not) pontificate on how Jesus endorses his personal worldview. He told us that what he wanted us to do was to gather for a meal. In *The Voyage of the Dawn Treader*,[40] King Caspian and his companions come to a far eastern island that celebrates a daily banquet. Every night the table fills with an unbeatable feast, and every morning birds arrive to eat whatever is left over. This abundance—where there is plenty for all and none goes to waste—reminds us of the feasts Isaiah envisioned, when God showed him the end of the world. This is the new heaven and the new earth, wherein we are invited to buy wine and milk without money and without price.[41] A sumptuous feast without end; in each earthly Eucharist we are permitted to join for a short time, a foretaste of what awaits us in future.

When we pray the Lord's Prayer (which we do at every Eucharist), we ask God to "give us this day our daily bread." This asks God to sustain us with the food we need, yes, but the ancient Church fathers taught that it also referred to the Eucharist. The Eucharist is medicine for penitent sinners; it is milk that strengthens babes and meat for strong warriors of God. Whether one partakes daily or weekly, many of us can feel, physically feel, a difference when we have gone long without the nourishment that is the very body and blood of Christ.

So what is the Eucharist? The Church as a whole differs, and the Episcopal Church dithers, when defining what precisely happens at the Holy Table of God. But we all agree that the Eucharist does five things:

Wait a minute, you *just said* that the Church community was the Body of Christ. How can Jesus be a person, a God, the Church, and bread, all at once? Well, magic. Jesus is present on his glorious throne in heaven, in the most blessed sacrament of the altar, and in the hearts of his faithful people all at the same time. Theologians have tried to explain this through various metaphors, but nothing completely captures it. My favorite metaphor is that of The Raven King in *Jonathan Strange and Mr Norrell*, who's present with Stephen Black and John Segundus at the same time he's with Strange and Norrell.

Thanksgiving to the Father

The very word "Eucharist" means thanksgiving, so the heart of the Eucharist is thankfulness for all of God's saving acts in history. As the old hymn says, "For love in creation, for heaven restored, for grace of salvation, O praise ye the Lord!"[42] God has given us so much, and at the altar, we return to him a sacrifice of praise and thanksgiving.

Memorial of the Son

In the Eucharist, this has a specific, sacramental, material meaning. We are not merely remembering the mighty acts of Christ, but also re-membering the Body of Christ. By telling the story, we make it real again. It is happening, again, while we tell it. It is made real and present by our saying it out loud.

Invocation of the Spirit

We invite the Spirit to come and sanctify the gifts of bread and wine, as well as the hearts of the gathered faithful. By inviting the Spirit to become Really Present among us in a way more than normal.

Communion of the Faithful

The community of those gathered in worship becomes one with Christ and with one another by partaking of the meal Christ left behind for us. The word "atonement" comes from the Old English and means "at-one-ment." In communion, we become one with God, and with all other partakers of the meal, both present locally and across the world.

Foretaste of the Kingdom

The most common metaphor for heaven shown to us in the Scriptures is a dinner party. No Hogwarts banquet can compare (not least because the heavenly banquet isn't cooked by house-elves, by order of SPEW).

 The **Society for the Promotion of Elfish Welfare** (SPEW) was an organization founded in 1994 by Hermione Granger in response to what she saw as gross injustice to the treatment of house-elves.

At most Episcopal churches, the primary Sunday worship is a eucharistic service. We believe that partaking often is essential for maintaining a right relationship with God and our neighbor. Some churches hold a daily Eucharist, and have members who keep a daily practice.

[Go to "The Adventure Path" on page 89 for an in-depth exploration of what you might experience if you were to attend the Sunday morning Eucharist at your nearest church.]

We have discussed how the Eucharist is a foretaste of the kingdom of heaven. But what is the kingdom of heaven? How will we know it? Let's explore:

The Kingdom of Heaven

At the end of his life, we believe, those who opposed the Jesus Movement exiled John the Apostle, the Evangelist, to the island of Patmos. There, he had a spectacular vision of the end of the world, the Second Coming of Jesus Christ, and the kingdom of heaven—"a new heaven and a new earth,"[43] he called it. This was written down by his followers and eventually included in the New Testament as the Revelation to John. Or maybe not—it could have all been an elaborate comeuppance metaphor arguing against the Roman dynasty currently in power. That "beast of the sea" he mentions? Probably the procurator of Asia Minor.

Regardless of the accuracy or intent of John's vision, Christians rightly focus on the kingdom of heaven. Jesus spoke about it often: "The kingdom of heaven has come near."[44] He told his disciples to proclaim that message to others. He taught us to pray for God's kingdom to come on earth, as in heaven.[45] But so often when Christians talk about heaven, we focus on a "place far away from here, where we go when we die, as opposed to hell, where Jesus saves us from going when we die." That's not how Jesus talked about it, at all, and we do our faith a disservice by reducing heaven in this way.

Think of the kingdom of heaven like Marion Zimmer Bradley's *The Mists of Avalon*,[46] where there's the Isle of the Priests (Glastonbury), and there's Avalon, the mystical isle that gradually pulls further and further away from our world. They sit on top of one another, and if you listen real hard, you can hear the chanting, the bells, voices from the other side of the veil. But they are not the same. Just so, the kingdom of heaven is here, on our world, now. But rather than pulling further and further away from us, Jesus is bringing it nearer and nearer.

This helps explain the "already but not yet" feeling that many believers have. Jesus proclaimed that "the kingdom of God has come to you,"[47] and Christians believe that Christ's time on earth inaugurated this gradual drawing together of heaven and earth. But we have only to watch the news or see how human beings treat one another to know that heaven is not here. Sin abounds. Tragedy persists. Cancer still kills, the good die young, and we hurt the ones we love. So while Jesus said that the kingdom of heaven has come near, he also promised to return one day—at a time when no one knows. And at his coming, all will finally be accomplished.

In other words, victory is assured, but it hasn't happened yet. Which is kind of a tangled mess of a time to live in. No wonder we all, including Christians, keep aggressively getting it wrong all the time. But it's an exciting time to live in too—a time when it is possible to partner with God in ministry. A time when we are invited to help make things as right as can possibly be. A time when what we do matters, when we can contribute to the fight.

Divisive Issues

This chapter has mostly dealt with the basics of Christian theology: who God is, who we are, and how God has chosen to interact with us. But when folks ask me about theology, often what they're looking for is a response to the "divisive issues" they read about in the news; that is to say, women's ordination and questions about acceptance of the LGBTQ+ community.

In commemorating one of the great seventeenth-century Anglican theologians, Richard Hooker, we pray that we might maintain a middle way, "not as a compromise for the sake of peace, but as a comprehension for the sake of truth."[48] When it comes to controversial topics, such as the ordination of women and LGBTQ+ persons, and marriage between persons of the same sex, the Episcopal Church strives to keep that comprehension—some would say to our detriment. Regardless of the advisability of this stance, the middle way is the road we have chosen, and you may meet Episcopalians who believe that marriage between persons of the same sex is a grave sin (though you're more likely to meet Episcopalians concerned that by permitting these marriages, we are harming our Anglican Communion and ecumenical relationships than Episcopalians who actually believe this is a sinful practice), just as you may meet Episcopalians at San Francisco Pride.

As for our theology as to why we ordain women: It is because we baptize little girls. When we are incorporated into the Body of Christ in baptism, all distinctions between us cease: There is neither Jew nor Greek, neither slave nor free, neither male nor female.[49] While there are certainly scriptural passages that indicate a limit to women's authority (1 Corinthians 11:3, 1 Timothy 2:11–12), there are others that show a surprising trust in women for the first century (Romans 16:1–2, 1 Corinthians 1:11, not to mention the fact that women are the sole witnesses to Christ's resurrection). Furthermore, if we were to accept the argument that because Christ became incarnate as a man, all the priests who serve him must be, then we must question the salvation of women. If it is Christ's masculinity and not his humanity that defines him, then the soul of every woman is in peril. Vampire Slayers may be only women, because it is through their actions and not their person that they save the world. But it is Christ's personhood that saves us, and if that personhood is uniquely and particularly masculine, then women are lost.

There are Episcopal women in leadership in every order of the Episcopal Church: laywomen, priests, deacons, and bishops. Because latent, systemic, unconscious sexism persists, there are fewer women than men serving as bishops and rectors of large churches. Very few churches and dioceses would claim a theological foundation for not calling women—indeed, very few would say that they are intentionally not calling women. This is an instance of sin [go to "Sin" on page 123] and it is something for which all of us (including women, who can internalize sexism as much as any man) must be on guard.

The question of whether homosexuality (that is, the identity) or "homosexual acts" is a sin is one that has occupied the Christian church for the last sixty years or more. Through over forty years of discernment, prayer, listening to the lived experience of gay, lesbian, bisexual, and transgender persons, and returning to the Scriptures for study, the Episcopal Church has determined that there is nothing inherently sinful about same-sex attraction. In so doing, we have recognized the sin of homophobia and heterosexism that has led the church to condemn LGBTQ+ persons for their relationships, their identities, their very beings.

Not everyone agrees, of course. There are still Episcopal dioceses where couples of the same sex cannot be married. There are still Episcopal congregations that struggle to welcome those whose gender expression doesn't conform to traditional expectations. But our theology is this: LGBTQ+ persons are created, as they are, their whole selves, in the image of God.

Conclusion

Leveling Up

In which the end is discovered to be a beginning

This book is meant as an introduction. Its purpose is to explain all those jargon-y Episcopal words, and to equip you to fully participate in worship at your local Episcopal church. But that's only a first step—level 1, the very beginning of building your character as a Christian. As you continue to glorify God and follow Christ, through the grace of the Holy Spirit, your XP will manifest not in power and influence, but in love, joy, peace, patience, kindness, generosity, faithfulness, gentleness, and self-control.[1]

But what is the next step? Whether you fancy yourself a caster, a fighter, a rogue, or a ranger, there are levels ahead for you. In order to reach them, the first thing you need to do is to find a church. It sucks that such a difficult step is so crucial, but it is. It doesn't much matter what *kind* of church, though you should definitely pick one you like enough that you'll keep going. It doesn't matter if you understand it, if you agree with what they say, if you're "behaving" well in your life—just go. Just being intentionally in the presence of God, spending time with a community that worships him, and regularly receiving the body of Christ in the Holy Eucharist has an effect. I would hesitate to quantify that effect—Lord knows churches are full of sinners—but something mystical happens to you in worship, no matter what you bring to it. So just show up, and let God work God's magic on you. Over time, you'll begin to see a more grace-filled, generous, merciful, humble self emerge.

Once you're worshipping regularly, you get to chart your own course. What part of the Christian adventure excites you most? You can dig into the community of Christians you've found and try to really support them in life: bringing them casseroles when they get a bad diagnosis, driving with them to spin class so you both are motivated to go, taking their call even when you can tell Sean Bean is about to die in the next ten minutes. This is called **pastoral care**, and it's the way that we love and support one another, embodying Jesus's care for the whole person. It's good for healer-y types, mostly, but adrenaline junkies might enjoy the "drop everything" aspects of it as well.

If pastoral care doesn't speak to you, you can try doing the work of what churches mostly call **outreach and mission**. This usually means outreach to the poor and needy, and doing the mission that Jesus outlines in Matthew 25: feeding the hungry, giving drink to the thirsty, clothing the naked, visiting the sick and the imprisoned, welcoming the stranger. There are two schools of thought here, and I endorse both of them. The first is the traditional idea of charity, from the Latin word *caritas*, or love. Charity gives with no expectation of return, because God first gave to us. Charity recognizes that those who have fewer worldly goods than we do could be us—we're just a few circumstances different. And so charity seeks to give to those in need, whether that gift takes the form of food, clothing, shelter, education, healthcare, or just straight-up cash (my preferred method of giving). In so doing, we offer to those in whom Christ is present the honor due to Christ himself.

This work can be done right in your own neighborhood, through volunteering to read to schoolchildren, serving dinner at a homeless shelter, or donating food (not your old nasty leftovers) to a food bank, or it can be done all across the world. Sometimes this work needs to be done in person, but other times, it just involves giving the money to the folks who distribute mosquito nets and deploy doctors. Do your research and support good organizations.

The second school of thought about mission and outreach is the promotion of justice. There's an old joke that's been applied to a number of saints and archbishops over time, and it goes like this: "When I feed the hungry, they call me a saint; when I ask why they are hungry, they call me a Communist."[2] Some Christians feel that charity, giving out of our largesse, is inadequate. Rather than just donating to a food bank, advocate for higher wages for local workers so that they needn't rely on food banks. Instead of shipping mosquito nets to Africa, get involved in the political process to encourage Western nations to forgive African debt, which could allow those nations to combat malaria on their own, without us standing over them. Get involved with Black Lives Matter protests, and demand that the government, which represents us all, respect the dignity of every human being. This, too, is outreach and mission, and it is essential to the work of the Church.

Being an Episcopalian, I'm a both/and kind of geek—we can both send mosquito nets to Africa and advocate for debt relief. We can pay anyone who works for us a proper, living wage instead of the least we can get away with (and encourage other boss-types to do the same) and still give to those who can't seem to make ends meet. This work, this outreach and mission work, seems to befit active-types the best: your fighters, your rangers, your boom-boom casters. People who enjoy less thinking, more doing.

If, however, you are less about the doing, and more about the thinking and the praying, then a more **contemplative** path is available to you. Traditionally, contemplatives have entered monastic orders—think Teresa of Avila, Julian of Norwich, Hildegard of Bingen, John of the Cross, Thomas Merton, and others. If you're called to that life, go for it. There are eighteen traditional orders and fourteen communities for men, women, or both in the Episcopal Church.

I'm not a monastic (and I'm not a contemplative type at *all*), but those who are tell me there are rich rewards that come with a life devoted to prayer and study in the quiet. The Church needs our contemplatives to pray for the rest of us, to study the Scriptures, to write and teach what they know, to offer hospitality and retreat for those of us who are in the world, and to serve the needy on a long-term basis and in a full-time kinda way (think Mother Teresa).

If you're not up for vows of poverty, chastity, and obedience, there are other options for a contemplative. The academe offers opportunities for solitude and study, learning and teaching. Many monastic orders have positions for associates who live according to a Rule of Life out in the world. Contemplation is not for the faint of heart, and it's a hard thing to do on your own. If you're not one for the monastic life, you should build a community around yourself to support you as you explore the mysteries of the universe and connect with God in a really intense and personal way. You should work through a couple levels before you try this life.

Another more advanced path is that of the **evangelist.** This role is for the folks my brother-in-law calls diplomancers—the PR arm of the Church, if you will. The reason I place this in the advanced category isn't because we don't all need to share our experience with Christ with others (indeed, we all do!), but because evangelists have done some pretty terrible things over the last, oh, 1,200 years or more.

The evangelist's job is to name the Holy where it is present, to build relationships with those outside the Church, to proclaim primarily by example what joy a life spent following Jesus can be. Evangelists should *not* shame, judge, correct, cajole, withhold love or material support from, or violently suppress those who follow God in another way, or who choose not to follow God at all. As Presiding Bishop Curry says, the goal of evangelism is not to conquer the world in the name of God. It is to saturate the world in love, to realize God's dream. If you feel tempted to disdain, mock, or otherwise put down those who disagree with you, the work of an evangelist is not for you. As Jesus said, "Whoever is not against you is for you"[3] Evangelism requires patience, generosity, openness to others, and an ability to hold disparate ideas in tension.

If none of these speak to you, there are other ways. John wrote that there was more to Jesus than could be contained in his Gospel,[4] and if he couldn't speak of all that following Christ offers, then I surely can't. Nor should you feel constrained by just one path. God calls us to do work for a time, then we might be asked to go on a new quest, with different requirements. If you are in regular worship with a community, have the support of other Christians, and are praying diligently, then you can captain your own quest. You can choose your own adventure.

So dive in. Here is water; what doth hinder you from being baptized? Die to sin, and rise anew to a life of following Jesus Christ. Further up and higher in, an ever-greater adventure awaits. So say we all, amen. Roll initiative!

Worlds Unknown
Addendum
In which n00bs can decipher the geek lingo

Angel A spinoff (1999–2004) of the TV series *Buffy the Vampire Slayer*, vampire Angel tries to get a fresh start in Los Angeles. Battling his own demonic nature, he joins forces with others to help the helpless and protect Angelenos from the demon threat. *www.secretsofangel.com*

Avatar: The Last Airbender An action-adventure TV series, film, and video games, the series follows the adventures of protagonist twelve-year-old Aang and his friends, who must bring peace and unity to the world by ending the Fire Lord's war against the other three nations. Set in an Asiatic-like world in which some people are able to manipulate the classical elements by use of psychokinetic variants of Chinese martial arts, known as "bending."

Battlestar Galactica An American science fiction franchise (books, movies, television series) begun in 1978 (but famously rebooted in 2009) that share the premise of a human civilization living in the distant part of the universe who are engaged in a lengthy war with a cybernetic race known as the Cylons. *www.syfy.com/battlestargalactica*

The Big Bang Theory An American sitcom on CBS centered on five characters living in Pasadena, California, two of whom are physicists who share an apartment and hang out with similarly geeky and social awkward friends. *www.cbs.com/shows/big_bang_theory*

Buffy the Vampire Slayer   A movie and television series about a young woman chosen for a specific mission: to seek out and destroy vampires, demons, and other forces of darkness and evil.
www.buffyworld.com

The Chronicles of Narnia   A series of seven high fantasy novels by British author C. S. Lewis (1950s) about four children who travel through a wardrobe to the land of Narnia, where they learn that they have been chosen to free the land from winter (evil) with the guidance of a mystical lion (Aslan).
https://narnia.com/

Dogma   A 1999 American dark comedy about two fallen angels who attempt to return to heaven after being cast out by God. Definitely pushes the buttons on the institutional church and the infallibility of God.

Doctor Who   A British science fiction television series produced since 1963, it features a doctor who is a space and time traveller. He explores the universe in his TARDIS, a time travelling machine, combatting a variety of adversaries along the way in his attempt to save civilizations.

Dragonriders of Pern   A science fiction series of twenty-two novels begun by Anne McCaffrey (1967) about a pre-industrialized civilization (Pern) that fights Thread, an agent that consumes organic material at a voracious rate, including crops, animals, and any humans in its path (kind of like Sin).

Dune   A 1965 epic science fiction novel by Frank Herbert that inspired a 1984 film and 2000 Sci-Fi Channel series. Set in the distant future amidst a feudal interstellar society, the story explores the multi-layered interactions of politics, religion, ecology, technology, and human emotion.
www.dunenovels.com

Dungeons & Dragons   Originally a fantasy tabletop role-playing game (RPG) developed in 1974 and now available online, each player takes on a character to play who embarks on an imaginary

adventure within a fantasy setting to engage in battles and build alliances while gaining knowledge and experience points.
www.ddo.com

Firefly   Set five hundred years in the future following a universal civil war, this American drama series is about disparate men and women trying to survive on the edge of a new frontier, like a modern, space western.
www.tv.com/shows/firefly/

Galaxy Quest   A 1999 American science fiction comedy that parodies 1970's sci-fi television shows such as "Star Trek." With an all-star cast, it has become a cult classic for those who enjoy intergalactic adventures.

Game of Thrones   George R.R Martin's best-selling book series "A Song of Ice and Fire" turned into an HBO medieval fantasy epic. Powerful families consisting of kings, queens, knights, spies, and renegades vie for control of the Seven Kingdoms of Westeros through several narrative arcs, all in an attempt to reclaim the throne while a rising threat of impending winter of destructive importance looms over all.
www.hbo.com/game-of-thrones

Hamilton   The Tony-award-winning Broadway musical about the life of American Founding Father Alexander Hamilton, with music, lyrics, and book by Lin-Manuel Miranda.
www.hamiltonbroadway.com

Harry Potter   A series of fantasy novels by J.K. Rowling that chronicle the life of a young wizard, Harry Potter, and his friends as they face the darker aspects of the human experience (Voldemort) and search for the meaning of wholeness and everlasting life.
www.pottermore.com

The Hunger Games   Suzanne Collins' 2008 dystopian trilogy about Katniss Everdeen's overthrow of the ruthless, wealthy Capitol that has power over the other twelve districts of people living in varying states of poverty.
www.scholastic.com/thehungergames/

Jonathan Strange and Mr. Norrell   A fantasy, historical drama TV miniseries (2015) based on the novel by Susanna Clark (2004) about the return of magic to England.

The Karate Kid   A 1984 American blockbuster that spun into sequels, this is an underdog story of a high school junior (Daniel) and his mentor, an aging Japanese immigrant. It is a story of friendship and overcoming adversity at the hands of bullies. "He taught him the secret to Karate lies in the mind and heart. Not in the hands."

The Lord of the Rings   Written from 1937 to 1949, this is an epic high-fantasy trilogy by British author J.R.R Tolkien. The three books consisting of *The Fellowship of the Ring, The Two Towers,* and *The Return of the King* were published from 1954 to 1955. Taking place in Middle Earth, the stories involve friendship, fantasy creatures, humans, and battles of good versus evil.
http://lotrproject.com

The Magicians   Based upon Lev Grossman's best-selling books, *The Magicians* centers around Brakebills University, a secret institution specializing in magic. There, amidst an unorthodox education of spellcasting, a group of twenty-something friends soon discover that a magical fantasy world they read about as children is all too real—and poses grave danger to humanity.
www.syfy.com/themagicians

Monty Python and the Holy Grail   A British cult classic (1975) of King Arthur and his knights embarking on a low-budget search for the Grail, the cup of Christ, in which they encounter obstacles, characters of all sorts, and biblical personalities.

Monty Python and the Life of Brian   (1979) features Brian, a contemporary of Jesus who is frequently mistaken as the Messiah.

The Mists of Avalon   A 1983 novel by Marion Zimmer Bradley, (turned into a TV miniseries in 2001) in which she relates the Arthurian legends from the perspective of the female characters.

O Brother, Where Art Thou?   A 2000 satiric adventure film of three prison escapees set in Mississippi during the Great Depression. Loosely based on Homer's *The Odyssey*, the characters search for freedom and hidden treasure while facing the perils of that time in our nation.

Outlander   A book series by Diana Gabaldon turned British-American television drama, it is an historical time travel epic of a World War II combat nurse (Claire) to the eighteenth century in the Highlands of Scotland (and back and forth between). *www.starz.com/series/outlander/episodes*

Pathfinder   A fantasy role-laying game (RPG) published in 2009 in the same style as *Dungeons & Dragons*, but with an open game license that allows the development of expansion systems to the game with more characters, monsters, and classes including game titles such as *Winter Witch* and *The Wizard's Mask*. *www.d20pfsrd.com*

PlayStation   Developed in Japan and released in 1994 by Sony Entertainment, PlayStation is a video game home console and handheld system, including PSX and other hardware. Popular games include *Doom, LEGO Star Wars: The Force Awakens, Mortal Kombat,* and *Minecraft*. *www.playstation.com/en-us/*

The Princess Bride   A fairy tale adventure movie (1973) about a beautiful young woman and her one true love. Based on the William Goldman novel of the same name, it is a story of a grandfather reading a story to his grandson in which he promises "Fencing. Fighting. Torture. Revenge. Giants. Monsters. Chases. Escapes. True Love. Miracles."

Raiders of the Lost Ark   Part of the Indiana Jones movie franchise, renowned archeologist and expert in the occult Dr. Indiana Jones sets out to find the Ark of the Covenant, believed to hold the ten commandments, before the Nazis can obtain it for their own power. Released in 1981. *The Last Crusade* (1989) finds Indiana searching for the Holy Grail (cup of Christ) before the Nazis (back again) can get their hands on it.

Redwall series   A series of children's fantasy novels by Brian Jacques (1986–2010). The characters in the books are all anthropomorphic animals; almost all of them can speak. The books are about the history of Redwall Abbey through time, involving good and evil plot lines. "Redwall is where safety and warmth surround you. Food, friends, music, and song. Redwall will always welcome you back."
www.redwall.org

Settlers of Catan   A multiplayer strategic board game developed in Germany in 1995 in which players assume the role of settlers in a new land, trading commodities and building communities with cities and knights.
www.catan.com

Star Trek   An American science fiction franchise (movie and television) that began in 1966 and continues with sequels and new generations. It follows the galactic adventures of James T. Kirk and the starship Enterprise and has become a cult phenomena and inspiration for several technological inventions including cell phones and tablet computers.
www.startrek.com

Star Wars   An American space epic and worldwide pop culture phenomenon, beginning with the release of the first film in 1977. In a fictional galaxy, the forces of good and evil are in constant conflict, with "the Force" being an omnipresent energy that can be harnessed by those with a special ability for good (the light side) or evil (the dark side).
www.starwars.com

The Tudors   A Showtime history-based dramas series of the young King Henry VIII that navigates the intrigues of the English court and the human heart.
www.sho.com/the-tudors

Notes

Introduction

1. Reinhold Niebuhr, quoted in James Cone, *The Cross and the Lynching Tree* (Maryknoll, NY: Orbis, 2013), 34.
2. J. K. Rowling, *Harry Potter and the Deathly Hallows* (New York: Arthur A. Levine, 2009), 328, and 1 Corinthians 15:26.
3. With a nod to *Hook*, Steven Spielberg's 1991 film starring Robin Williams as a grown-up Peter Pan who returns to Neverland.

Introduction 2.0

1. Courtesy of Wash in the *Firefly* pilot.

The Hero

1. *Buffy the Vampire Slayer*. Created by Joss Whedon, performance by Sarah Michelle Gellar, Mutant Enemy, 1997–2003. Opening credits.
2. Tolkien's Catholicism is well documented and permeates *The Lord of the Rings* trilogy.
3. Whedon is outspokenly atheist but nonetheless explores faith throughout his TV series *Buffy the Vampire Slayer*, *Angel*, and *Firefly* and films such as *The Avengers*.
4. Genesis 1:1, John 1:1.
5. In the TV series *Angel*, there are The Powers That Be, godlike characters who help our protagonists out.
6. Okay, so it's not exactly like Harry and Voldemort's prophecy (in *Order of the Phoenix*), but just go with me here.

The Ultimate Quest

1. 2 Corinthians 5:16–20.
2. Romans 5:8.
3. Howard Thurman's most famous work is called *Jesus and the Disinherited* (Boston: Beacon Press, 1996), which builds to this thesis.
4. Micah 4:4. Yes, Hamilfans, George Washington really did quote it a lot.
5. "One Last Time," *Hamilton*, Lin-Manuel Miranda.

The Player's Handbook: A Rudimentary Guide to the Book of Common Prayer

1. Flashback to NBC's old PSAs. We're getting way too into the details here.
2. From the Preface of the 1789 Book of Common Prayer, as printed in *The Book of Common Prayer* (New York: Seabury, 1979), 11. [Hereafter referred to as BCP.]
3. Although Rite I Holy Eucharist retains much of this Elizabethan language.
4. À la *Reading Rainbow*. *www.readingrainbow.com*
5. Sing along with me and Julie Andrews in *The Sound of Music*.
6. Godly Play is a particular style of early childhood Christian formation, using Montessori principles. Learn more at *www.godlyplayfoundation.org*.
7. See *The Magicians* series, by Lev Grossman. *http://levgrossman.com/magicians-trilogy/*
8. Image courtesy of "Mhysa," season 3, episode 10 of *Game of Thrones*.
9. Diana Gabaldon, *Outlander* (New York: Dell, 1992), 576.
10. Acts 8:36, KJV.
11. BCP, 335.
12. Thank you, *The Princess Bride*.
13. BCP, 423.
14. Canon 18, as amended at the 78th General Convention in 2015, Resolution A036.
15. BCP, 331.
16. James 5:14.
17. You know, those alien guys from *Galaxy Quest* (RIP Alan Rickman).

Classes: The Orders of Ministry

1. Acts 8:36, KJV.
2. Acts 10:48.
3. Psalm 110:4, Hebrews 7:17.
4. C. S. Lewis, *Mere Christianity* (San Francisco: HarperSanFrancisco, 2001 edition).
5. Acts 6:1.
6. George Herbert, "King of Glory," *The Hymnal 1982* (New York: Church Hymnal, 1982), hymn 382.
7. Stephen Ministry is the one-to-one lay caring ministry that takes place in congregations the use the Stephen Series program system. *www.stephenministries.org*
8. As named in the Prayers of the People.
9. Channeling Samuel L. Jackson in *Snakes on a Plane*.
10. BCP, 543.
11. BCP, 543.

12. BCP, 531.

13. Hebrews 7:17.

14. Forbidden from performing any sacraments, or holding oneself out as a priest. Can be temporary.

15. Jeremiah 23:1, Ezekiel 34:2.

16. Bishophood.

17. "Putting in order."

18. "Making sacred."

19. BCP, 517.

20. BCP, 517.

21. Philippians 2:6–8.

Vestments: The Cosplay Section of Church

1. Those who play in live action role-playing games (LARP).

2. Matthew 11:30.

Equipment: Fire and Big Sticks

1. Identified by a seven-hundred-year-old knight waiting to be relieved of his watch over the Grail to Indiana Jones.

2. Psalm 51:10, BCP, 656.

The Adventure Path: Let's Go to Church

1. Suzanne Collins, *The Hunger Games* (New York: Scholastic, 2008).

2. In the twenty-seventh of his 95 *Theses*, Martin Luther attributes this claim to Johann Tetzel; the Catholic Encyclopedia disputes.

3. BCP, 360.

4. Isaiah 6:1–8.

5. Philippians 4:7 and BCP, 339.

Comic-Con Lite: The General Convention

1. George Washington's Farewell Address, as quoted in "One Last Time" from the musical *Hamilton*.

2. Kevin Costner and James Earl Jones bring heaven to Iowa in *Field of Dreams* (1989).

3. *http://www.episcopalarchives.org*

4. With a shout out to Lin-Manuel Miranda of *Hamilton* (the musical) fame, whom you've noticed is very present in this chapter.

5. The Diocese of Virginia is one of the biggest (in terms of congregations) dioceses in the church, well known for throwing awesome parties.

6. A Eucharist celebrating the contributions of LGBTQ+ persons to God's church. *http://www.integrityusa.org*

7. Traditionally on Tuesday night, all the seminaries of the Episcopal Church hold dinners to celebrate their alumni. *www.episcopalchurch.org/page/episcopal-seminaries*

8. *www.acts8movement.org*

9. *www.episcopalchurch.org/page/united-thank-offering*

10. *www.episcopalrelief.org*

Magic: The God Part

1. Susanna Clarke, *Jonathan Strange and Mr Norrell: A Novel* (New York: Tor Books, 2006).

2. Lev Grossman, *The Magicians: A Novel (Magician's Trilogy)* (New York, Penguin Books, 2010).

3. Lyle W. Dorsett, *The Essential C. S. Lewis* (New York: Simon and Schuster, 1996), 43. C. S. Lewis's Mr. Beaver telling Susan about Aslan in *The Lion, the Witch, and the Wardrobe*.

4. Matthew 5:45.

5. BCP, 218.

6. Romans 6:3–8.

7. 1 Corinthians 15:53–54.

8. 1 Corinthians 12:13.

9. Aka *Firefly's* "universe."

10. Paul Atriedes in *Dune* by Frank Herbert (Radnor, PA: Chilton Book Company, 1965), 8.

11. Shankar Vedantam and Krys Boyd, "Our Unconscious Minds," THINK, January 27, 2010. An NPR show featuring in-depth interviews with compelling guests, covering a wide variety of topics ranging from history, politics, current events, science, technology, adventure, and entertainment. *www.kera.org/radio/think/*

12. Matthew 5:22.

13. Matthew 7:5.

14. John 8:7.

15. 1 John 1:8.

16. 2 Corinthians 12:9.

17. 1 John 1:9.

18. Genesis 1:27.

19. Colossians 1:15.

20. Psalm 19:1.

21. "Stars" from *Les Miserables*, Boublil and Schonberg's 1980 musical.

22. Psalm 8.

23. Genie is the tritagonist in Disney's 1992 animated feature film *Aladdin*. Read more about him at *http://disney.wikia.com/wiki/Genie*

24. A nod of the head to my fellow Whovians.

25. John 1:29.

26. Luke 2:41–52.

27. Matthew 14:13–21, Mark 6:30–44, Luke 9:10–17.

28. BCP, 339.

29. C. S. Lewis, *The Lion, the Witch, and the Wardrobe* (London: Geoffrey Bles, 1950).

30. J.K. Rowling, *Harry Potter and the Deathly Hallows* (New York: Scholastic, 2007), 692.

31. James H. Cone. *The Cross and the Lynching Tree* (Maryknoll, NY: Orbis Books, 2011).

32. Romans 12:17–21.

33. Acts 2:1–4.

34. The main religion of the Seven Kingdoms in *Game of Thrones*.

35. BCP, 867.

36. At least, Bobby McFerrin does.

37. Mark 9:40.

38. Matthew 22:37–39, Mark 12:29–31, Luke 10:27.

39. Given during her address at the *Why Christian?* conference, September 30, 2015 in Minneapolis.

40. C. S. Lewis. *The Voyage of the "Dawn Treader"* (New York: Harper Collins, 1952).

41. Isaiah 65:17, 55:1.

42. Henry Williams Baker, "O Praise Ye the Lord," *The Hymnal 1982* (New York: Church Hymnal, 1982), hymn 432.

43. Revelation 21:1.

44. Matthew 3:2.

45. Matthew 6:10.

46. Marion Zimmer Bradley. *The Mists of Avalon* (New York: The Ballantine Publishing Group, 1982).

47. Luke 11:20.

48. *Lesser Feasts and Fasts* (New York: Church Publishing, 2006), 415.

49. Galatians 3:28.

Conclusion: Leveling Up

1. The "fruits of the Spirit" as outlined by Paul in his letter to the Galatians 5:22–23.
2. Attributed to former Brazilian archbishop Dom Hélder Câmara, among others.
3. Luke 9:50.
4. John 20:30–31.

www.ingramcontent.com/pod-product-compliance
Lightning Source LLC
Jackson TN
JSHW011402130125
77033JS00023B/808